Pomegranate Seeds

JEWISH LATIN AMERICA
Ilán Stavans, series editor

Mestizo: A Novel by Ricardo Feierstein

The Jewish Gauchos of the Pampas by Alberto Gerchunoff

Cláper: A Novel by Alicia Freilich

The Book of Memories by Ana María Shua

The Prophet and Other Stories by Samuel Rawet

The Fragmented Life of Don Jacobo Lerner by Isaac Goldemberg

*Passion, Memory, and Identity: Twentieth-Century
Latin American Jewish Women Writers,* edited by Marjorie Agosín

*King David's Harp: Autobiographical Essays
by Jewish Latin American Writers,* edited by Stephen A. Sadow

The Collected Stories of Moacyr Scliar by Moacyr Scliar

Sun Inventions and *Perfumes of Carthage* by Teresa Porzecanski

Losers and Keepers in Argentina by Nina Barragan

*The Martyr: Luis de Carvajal:
A Secret Jew in Sixteenth Century Mexico* by Martin Cohen

Like a Bride and *Like a Mother* by Rosa Nissán

Secrecy and Deceit: The Religion of the Crypto-Jews by David M. Gitlitz

The Algarrobos Quartet by Mario Goloboff

1492 by Homero Aridjis

*Yiddish South of the Border: An Anthology
of Latin American Yiddish Writing,* edited by Alan Astro

Unbroken: Testimony of a Holocaust Survivor in Buenos Aires by Charles
Papiernik, translated from the Spanish by Stephen A. Sadow

The Letters That Never Came by Mauricio Rosencof,
translated from the Spanish by Louise B. Popkin

Pomegranate Seeds

Latin
American
Jewish Tales

NADIA GROSSER NAGARAJAN

Introduction by Ilán Stavans

University of New Mexico Press
Albuquerque

Dedicated to the memory

of my beloved parents

Bedrich and Aranka Grosser

© 2005 by the University of New Mexico Press
Introduction © 2005 by Ilán Stavans.
All rights reserved. Published 2005
Printed and bound in the United States of America
09 08 07 06 05   1 2 3 4 5

LIBRARY OF CONGRESS CATALOGING-IN-PUBLICATION DATA

Nagarajan, Nadia Grosser.
Pomegranate seeds : Latin American Jewish tales / Nadia Grosser
Nagarajan.— 1st ed.
p. cm. — (Jewish Latin America)
ISBN 0-8263-2391-x (pbk. : alk. paper)
1. Jews, Latin American—Folklore.
2. Folklore—Latin America.
3. Latin America—Social life and customs.
I. Title. II. Series. GR98.N27 2005
398.2'089'92408—dc22
2004017462

DESIGN AND COMPOSITION: *Mina Yamashita*

Contents

Contents

vi

Preface

$\mathcal{I}$ had a dream the other night. I was walking uphill along a winding trail and found a pomegranate on the ground. The rind was hard and slightly cracked in a few places as if at any time it was going to burst. It glowed with a deep golden-red color and the scarlet flower at its end had already withered since the fruit was very ripe. When I picked it up, it broke open and hundreds of crimson seeds rolled in all directions. They all had the typical ruby-red hue but their sizes were not uniform, their shapes not exactly even; a few ruptured while most of them remained intact; still others had dried out and were brownish and shrunken. I gathered a few of these kernels in my hand and woke up. It occurred to me then that the tales in this book are just like the seeds I found in my dream. They comprise a cluster of stories that have been dispersed in various directions during the course of Jewish history. Although they are just a sample of countless told and untold narratives, they are symbolic representatives of the singular fortitude of the Jewish spirit. These tales, except for the two retold from material found in the Israel Folktale Archives, are based on the interviews, conversations, and unforgettable encounters I have had with many strangers whom I met along the way and who since then have become my friends.

The road I have taken in search of Jewish folktales in Latin America has been long, strenuous, and tiring, but at the end rewarding and fulfilling. The exceptional fiction created by many Jewish authors in the Latin American hemisphere over the years has provided an additional dimension to the history of Jewish Literature, yet the simple folktales and cultural oral narratives that are a basic legacy of the Jewish people have not been a part of it. I started my journey in search of them strengthened by my belief that there were many hidden treasures to be found in that part of the world that had not been uncovered over the years due to many factors such as disinterest, forgetfulness, or just the mere fact that it has been assumed that the Jews of South America and the Caribbean Basin did not have any tales, old or new, like those of their European and Middle Eastern brethren. My will to pursue this project was based not only on my lifelong interest in folklore and my heritage in particular, but can also be attributed to my deep affection for Latin America and its people in general.

This book is the result of extensive research, lengthy travel, and a large number of interviews and encounters. At first I followed the traditional path exploring archives, libraries, and associations—academic and non-academic institutions in the United States and abroad that I hoped would have material pertaining to the oral history and folklore of the Jews in Latin America. I was looking for tales recorded not only from the Ashkenazi perspective, but from the Sephardic and Oriental as well. I also contacted representatives of organizations, communities, and synagogues in many South and Central American countries as well as the Caribbean Islands. Finally, I reached out to a large number of private people whom I had found along trails pointed out to me by many friends, friends of friends and their contacts, as well as some of the institutions I had been in touch with earlier.

Along the way I experienced disappointment but also great satisfaction. The disillusionment was due to my initial enthusiastic expectations and, probably, also naive belief that I could easily find a substantial oral and recorded Jewish heritage in the Latin American continent, which proved to be wrong. I realized that, for the most part, resources were scarce and very little effort had been invested in preserving the past, as people were too busy safe-guarding their lives and properties, particularly in places where Jews were not welcome. The absence of concern among the young also contributed to the fact that records and documents were discarded over the years and events forgotten and dismissed. However, during this journey I discovered that I had also been right in assuming that, despite the facts mentioned above, many Jewish traditions of the past are still alive and throbbing under the dust accumulated over long periods of time. It was a matter of removing the dirt and uncovering hidden treasures underneath. And, thus, I was able to find tales that feed on their European roots and others that also extract from the past but do reflect the influence of life in the new hemisphere. Some stories are, in a way, a continuation of a very old tradition that goes back to pre-Colombian Spain. I discovered tales concealed by tropical greenery, encircled by vast jungles and flowing majestic rivers that echo many voices and reflect many views and visions. They represent people who, although true to their Jewish calling, had to adjust to new ways of life in order to survive. Some of these stories have the narrative structure and occasional motif that will qualify them as folklore rather than oral accounts of actual happenings. Many have to do with personal feelings, emotional insights, and interpretations of the protagonists. Others deal with happy or traumatic events that cannot be forgotten, and dreams that have not been fulfilled. National, geographic, secular, and religious preferences are present and reflect certain needs of the human soul. Various influences such as heritage, tradition, local customs and habits are evident, and in some of the stories the physical landscape also has a deep effect on the people. It seems to me that, despite the obvious outside influences, the tales in one way or another—for better or for worse—contain values that are specific to the spirit of the Jewish people. The stories are not arranged according to any particular genre or theme since many of them defy classification altogether. Just like the dispersed pomegranate seeds, they all come from a common cluster, yet each is a kernel in its own right.

The interviews were conducted in many different locations in the various countries I visited. I was touched by the generosity with which most of the people opened their hearts to me and shared their memories, anecdotes, and life experiences. I have retold the stories—that at times were only fragments, scraps of real incidents mingled with perhaps some fantasy, or sketchy and detached remembrances—creating a background when necessary so that the tales come to life as distinct entities.

By no means have I exhausted this treasure. I had to stop at a certain point since I had only my own limited private resources but do believe that there is still a lot to explore and find in many places of the Latin American continent as well as Central America and the Caribbean

Basin. The magic of the unknown might cast its spell on others who will continue searching for more seeds of the lost pomegranate. Numerous tales, unfortunately, will be gone forever since those who are old, and have not had a chance to share them with others, will take them to their graves. Hopefully, though, some will survive in the memory of their descendants. One of my new friends in Manaus, in the depths of the Brazilian jungle, always sends me a gigantic, heartfelt Amazonian hug, which seems to encompass the world. I would like to share it with all the people I met during my long journey who helped in my search and told me their tales.

Acknowledgments

I extend sincere gratitude to Ilán Stavans who supported my idea for this project and agreed to write the introduction, to Howard Schwartz who encouraged me in this endeavor following my earlier book, *Jewish Tales from Eastern Europe*, to Peninnah Schram, Cherie Karo Schwartz, and Corinne Stavish for their friendship, interest in my work, and help in finding contacts. Many thanks to the University of New Mexico Press for publishing this book and including it in their prestigious Judaica Series, and to David Holtby, Mina Yamashita, Peter Matta, and Glenda Madden for their valuable help in the production process. My deep appreciation goes to my husband who traveled with me, cheered me up during days of doubt and disappointment, and clarified and enriched my ideas with his comments and observations, and to my sons, Ravi and Amith, whose encouragement and undivided attention benefited me greatly.

I would like to express my heartfelt tribute to the people whose names are listed according to the countries they live in, or where they originally dwelt; they provided connections in different Latin American locations and enabled me to find many useful sources. In addition, I mention the names of those on whose interviews the tales are based at the end of each narrative. Finally, I would like to stress that every single person I was in contact with, interviewed, and/or met during this memorable journey contributed to the attainment of my objective as I was doing research or traveling, and to my inspiration while writing the stories.

United States of America Elsa Altshool, Michele Anish, Rabbi Melanie Aron, Arthur Benveniste, Rabbi Marcelo Bronstein, Denise Chavez, Hugo D. de Castro Salas, Marta Felcman, Sara Ghitis, Mary McVey Gill, Yael A. Golton, Alberto Grosmark, David G. Hirsh, Stan Hordes, Hana Josephy, Samuel Kahn, Rabbi Gerald Kane, Elaine Klein, Jeanette Kleinberg, Jose Kleinberg, Carolyn Kunin, Seth Kunin, Sita Likuski, Rabbi Alejandro Lilienthal, Al Mizrahi, Simon Murray, Leah Orent, Rosa Perla Resnick, Daniel Radzinski, Stephen A. Sadow, Edward Samiljan, Rabbi Dennis Sasso, Rabbi Sandy Sasso, Alberto Socolovsky, Saul Sosnowski, Dana Vago

Argentina Armando Bublik, Rosa Pelisch de Jasin, Norma Salomon de Malamud, Myriam Diner, Adolfo Gass, Abraham Huberman, Ana Maria Karszenbaum, Isaías Leo Kremer, David Nul, Esther Schwartz,

Jose Tarica, Ana Tarnaruder, Eliahu Toker, Rabbi Felipe Yafe

Bolivia Olga Greguskova

Brazil Gabriele Becker, Jorge Bentes, Rabbi Nilton Bonder, Alice Brill, Juljan Czapski, Isaac Dahan, Fanny Kon, Ilana Halina Maria Kraus, Diane Kuperman, Rabbi Sergio Margulies, Margarida de Souza Neves, Laura Oru Semo Rosen, Rachel Rosenblum, Ariella Pardo Segre, Liliana Wajnberg, Goan T. and Fernanda Yo, Andre Zalcman

Canada Susana Singer Lombardi

Chile Adriana Balter, Camila Benado, Jacques Ergas Benmayor, Jose Chame, Bruno Contreras, Ana Maria Barrechea Grunwald de Lawner, Dolly Grunwald Steiner de Sitniski, Marita Feldmann, Rabbi Roberto Feldmann, Moises Hasson, Sylvia Tita Lawner Kaplan, Isidoro Basis Lawner, Jorge Sitniski Lawner, Juan Manuel y Ana Maria Volosky Lawner, Raul Sitniski Lawner, Rebeca Basis Lawner, Maxine Lowy, Guillermo y Cecilia Preminger, Jose Manuel Rivera, Jorge Zuniga Rodrigues, Washington Domb Scott, Lezat Shallat, Esther Lawner Steiman, Humberto Silva, Miguel Lawner Steiman, Wilhelm Stern, Gladys Rodriguez Valdes

Colombia Simon Brainsky

Curacao Lucille Berry-Haseth, Joan Capriles, Rosemary de Paula, Eunice Delvalle, Charles Gomes-Casseres, Diane Henriquez, Edsel (Papy) Jesurun, Rene D.L. Maduro, Nadya Moron, Michele Russel-Capriles

Ecuador Kurt Dorfzaun, Henry Horvath, Pedro Katz, Sergio Solon

Israel Yishayahu Birnbaum, Aaron Bukspan, Eli Bukspan, Hana Dukas, Edna Hechal, Raphael Schutz, Ariel Segal, David Sherf, Teodoro Socolovsky, Yehonathan Sorek

Panama Graciela Podest Cardoze, David de Castro, Hector de Lima, Ralph de Lima Valencia, Gloria Halman, Anita Henriquez, Milton C. Henríquez, Milton Henriquez Sr., Richard Holzer, Salomon Klaczko, Julieta and Johny Maduro and family, Ernesto Motta, Eleanor Perkins, Cheryl Pinto, David Robles, Colman A. Sasso, Rita Sasso, Carlos Valencia

Peru Eva Silverman Aleman, Rabbi Guillermo Bronstein, Rosalinda Loebl de Peck, Armando Peck Fishman, Jacobo Kapilivsky, Shabtai Stein, Leon Trahtemberg, Isaac Vainstein, Tania Vainstein, Hozkel Vurnbrand

Uruguay Teresa Porzecanski

Venezuela Genie Lubowski de Spiess, Alicia Freilich, Margot Labunsky, Rebeca Perli, Armando Quintero, Warren Spiess

Introduction

ILÁN STAVANS

*M*y copy of Nathan Ausubel's *A Treasury of Jewish Folklore* is falling apart. I've entered and exited the book with such regularity it has almost lost its binding. Its almost 750 pages are hypnotizing to me. They contain anonymous legends, humor, wisdom, songs, and stories about *schnorers* [plural Yiddish noun for a beggar who shows wit, brass, and resourcefulness], *shlemiels* [a clumsy, inept person], and *shlimazls* [a luckless fellow] dating as far back as the Bible and as recent as World War II. The anthology was published in 1948 although I see that the copyright in the copy I have was renewed in 1975. It also says that the publisher has gone back to press forty-eight times since the renewal. This means that there are thousands and thousands of copies around.

Why so popular? The answer is simple: it gives voice to the people. Ausubel wasn't a sophisticated scholar. The sources he mentions for the hundreds of tales gathered are almost always incomplete. Yes, each section has a preface placing themes in context and the structure of the anthology is excellent. Plus, there is a glossary explaining terms like *Gehenna* [hell] and *Shem-hamforesh* [the tetragramaton, the sacred name of God]. But readers interested in the depth of Ausubel's research are invariably disappointed. How did he get this wealth of information? How long did it take him? His seven-page introduction is infuriating: in it he talks about the *Midrash* as a favorite channel for Jewish wisdom; yet aside from a passing reference to himself at the beginning ("I was motivated by the desire to recapture the fading memory of the wonder and beauty that had inspired my childhood in the Old World"), he hardly ever explains how he himself came about the endeavor. Nor does he give the reader any autobiographical reference to understand his own priorities. However, as years go by I have come to the realization that this is an asset: Ausubel wants to disappear as editor; his mission, it seems to me, is to let the material speak for itself, as it does in the Talmud. The roots of the project matter little. He wants various rabbinical voices belonging to different time and place to speak to one another, to inhabit a continuum where past, present, and future become one.

Other books have embarked on the same effort Ausubel chose, most recently Howard Shwartz's voluminous *Tree of Souls: The Mythology of Judaism*. Indeed, the quest to collect Jewish legends is part of an early nineteenth-century pedagogical undertaking of the German thinker Leopoldo Zunz known as *Wissenschaft des Judentums*, the scientific investigation of Judaism. Zunz, an advocate of social reform who died in 1886, was a product of the Enlightenment. He wanted to understand Jewish literature, including its liturgy, not through the Talmudic debates that populated it but by paying attention to folklore. The word *folklore* has a German etymology: it makes reference to the traditional beliefs, legends, and customs current among the populace. By World War II, the idea of an omnibus of Jewish lore was quite fashionable among intellectuals. In fact, it had moved from the general to the specific. Some scholars concentrated on biblical mythology while others might do so on the Hellenistic period, the Middle Ages, Christian Spain, the mystical tradition, etc. The *Sefer Ha-Aggadah*, edited by Hayim Nahman Bialik and Yehoshua Hana Ravnitzky, is an offspring of Zunz's endeavor, and so is Shmuel Yosef Agnon's *Days of Awe*. One might also include in this list Martin Buber's compendium of Hasidic tales, although the best, by far most accomplished example is Louis Ginzberg's magisterial multi-volume *The Legends of the Jews*. Ginzberg taught for more than fifty years at The Jewish Theological Seminary. He wrote these studies in German, using rabbinic *Midrash* and classical tales.

In spite of its shortcomings—above all, it strives to please mainstream audiences—Ausubel's *A Treasury of Jewish Folklore* has a special place in my heart, for reasons I might be able to explain only partially. Over the years I've tried to find out more about Ausubel beyond the succinct information offered in back covers. He was born in Austria in 1899 and came to the United States at the age of eight, eventually becoming an American citizen. He translated the work of Sholem Asch (the novel *The Mother*, among others), but is primarily known as the editor responsible for other omnibuses: *A Treasury of Jewish Humor* and *A Treasury of Jewish Poetry*, among them, released in 1951 and 1957 respectively. He also produced, in the interregnum, always with the New York house Crown, a *Pictorial History of the Jewish People*. It is obvious to me that my empathy with Ausubel has to do with my own interest in "portable libraries," as I've described the Jewish anthologies I've edited since the nineties, starting with *Tropical Synagogues*. There is a legitimate educational need—and recreational too, of course—for these types of volumes. They approach literature, no matter its type, emphasizing the circumstance in which it sprung to light. But they also do a couple of other services: they offer a compass, allowing the reader to build bridges across individuals and cultures; plus, they force us to see authorship less as a solipsistic adventure and more as part of a larger succession of events. Our self is part of a never-ending flux of talent that has neither a beginning nor an end. Our beliefs and thoughts are part of a larger plan. Our self is less unique than we might imagine; it is but one in an infinite sequence of manifestations of a higher Spirit, an Author of Author whose machinations are not lessened with repetition.

When Nadia Grosser Nagarajan, responsible for *Jewish Tales from Eastern Europe*, contacted me with the informal proposal to collect an assortment of Jewish Latin American folk tales, I responded with enthusiasm. This region of the world contains the fifth largest concentration of Jews—after the United States, Israel, the former Soviet Block, and France—yet it remains the most eclipsed. Only in the last three decades has research into its history, folklore, traditions, and customs gathered some stamina. Jewish life in these territories started in the colonial period, with the arrival of crypto-Jewish and New Christians in Columbus's caravels. An Ashkenazic immigration took hold as the age of nationalism was sweeping across Europe and *pogroms* in places like Poland and the Ukraine were becoming more and more frequent. Then came yet another immigration wave, this one with Sephardic ancestry, from Syria, Lebanon, and northern Africa. What would tales about Gauchos and *shlemiels* be like? Could one imagine a version of "The Tale of the Cave of Simeon bar Yohai" set in the Amazon jungle? How about legends on the coming of the Messiah among an orthodox group in Cochabamba? Are there variations of the Hershele Ostropolyer stories, essentially the Jewish equivalent of the Hispanic archetypal rascal Juan Urdemalas, adapted into the Caribbean idiosyncrasy? (The only similar attempt I'm acquainted with is by the Guatemalan writer Alcina Lúbitch Domecq.) How about locating *Gehenna* in a Havana prison? Could one visualize a series of proverbs and maxims attributed to Rabbi Marshal T. Meyer from Buenos Aires?

Deep inside me I knew Nagarajan, in her pursuit, would face insurmountable hurdles. Archival and scholarly institutions devoted to Jewish historiography from Mexico to Argentina are still in their infancy in terms of development. In many ways it is as if the echoes of *Wissenschaft des Judentums* had not yet reached these shores. Only in the last couple of decades have museums focusing on Jewish settlements been established. In the Pampa the tourist today might visit Moisésville, a commune where Yiddish-speaking dwellers from *shtetls* in Europe relocated in the 1880s thanks to the financial support of philanthropists like Baron Maurice de Hirsch and organizations like the Alliance Israelite Universelle. In downtown Mexico City the facilities in Calle Justo Sierra where the Ashkenazic community had its gravitational center, in religious and cultural terms, are available upon request. But these sites have been arranged for foreigners with a modicum of historical knowledge. A generation of scholars is still being formed capable of offering a context through which to understand the plight of this diverse minority south of the Rio Grande. The little regard for Jewish material in Latin America is nothing short of appalling. Would it sound too melodramatic if I make reference to my not infrequent loss of sleep thinking of the wealth of data—personal diaries about the Holocaust and its connection to Latin America, newspapers in Yiddish and Ladino, Bar Mitzvah photographs, religious paraphernalia (menorahs, dreidls, Purism *shpiels*), impromptu liturgy, etc.—discharged at a regular basis in urban centers alone like Sao Paolo, Caracas, and Bogotá?

Fortunately, Nagarajan didn't give up easily. As she states in her preface, she benefited in part from the Israel Folklore Archive in Haifa but in the end decided to take another route: the oral tradition. She interviewed people from around the world with connections to the region, from Bolivia to Chile, from Canada the United States. She came up with almost three dozen delicious tales that, in scores of ways, are a reverberation of those found in Ausubel's *A Treasury of Jewish Folklore*. They are evidence of the cross-pollinations of Jewish, Christian, and pre-Columbian (Mapuche, Quechua) viewpoints. There are Midrashim that return to archetypes like the discerning rabbi and the lost child. A communion between the earthly and the spiritual realms is established. Some are about Nazis and refugees and about *conversos*. More than a handful are set in Argentina, but Curaçao, Brazil, Bolivia, and Costa Rica, among others, also serve as stage. The Ashkenazic and Sephardic identities are also explored. In the past years I've reread the oeuvre of Isaac Bashevis Singer, who left us with more than three hundred stories for adults and children, aside from his novels like *The Slave* and *Shadows in the Hudson* and the memoirs included in *Love and Exile*. Singer is an extraordinarily successful storyteller because he mastered the art of delivering a tale with charm and suspense. His reservoir of images and vocabulary is enviable. But he was something else too: a committed listener of other people's tales. He frequented cafeterias in New York City where all sorts of displaced individuals like him waited for life to give them a chance. And while they waited they told each other stories. Singer paid attention to them and then reshaped what they told into compelling tales of love, revenge, and the supernatural. Nagarajan is also a conscientious listener. In this volume, she models herself after Leopold Zunz: as a compiler of beliefs, legends, and customs, and as a conduit that lets the collective psyche speak for itself. To the best of my knowledge, she is the first person ever to contemplate these simultaneous roles in connection with the Jews of Latin America. This makes her a veritable pioneer. Like Singer, she has invested time and energy to let these voices out. And like Ausubel, to the extent that is possible she also—more often than not—wants to disappear as an editor.

I must confess: her quest has inspired me through and through. I now dream of one day spending an entire year, perhaps more, wandering from both sides of the U.S.–Mexican border to the Patagonia, exploring the labyrinthine selves of crypto-Jews in Arizona and Colorado, studying the effects of the Holy Office of the Inquisition from the seventeenth century on in the Americas, reflecting on the pogrom of 1919 known as *Semana trágica*, exposing myself to Yiddish tangos in Entre Ríos, eating *latkes* in Porto Alegre, and appreciating the humor that results from the Jewish and the Hispanic and Portuguese worlds as they collide. I visualize an ambitious book, part history, part travelogue, part a survey of folk ways, that benefits from direct, personal experience while making the shared experience of almost half a million people become not only tangible but urgent. This endeavor, now I see, justifies who I am, where I've been, and what I strive for. I hope it isn't only a dream of mine but part of God's vast plan. Meanwhile, I look forward to the day when, in an expanded edition of Ausubel's *A Treasury of Jewish Folklore*, tales like the ones Nadia Grosser Nagarajan delivers are incorporated, intertwined with their counterparts from other corners of the globe. That alone would somehow announce an end to the eclipse that keeps the Jews of Latin America unattended as a field of scholarship. I also hope to live to see a brigade of researchers, with Nagarajan's anthology perhaps also falling apart from use, descending into these communities to appraise the material culture before it is too late, producing scholarship that will sit in the shelves along Bialik, Ginzberg, and Agnon. I for one know scores of Spanish- and Portuguese-speaking *schnorers* and *shlimazls* whose adventures, unrecorded still, are the stuff of legend.

I Only Did that which My God Required

The Story of the American Schooner *Cohannit*

On a gloomy October day in 1877, night fell early on the town of Cumana, located at the Gulf of Cariaco that separates the peninsula of Araya from the rest of Venezuela. David Haim Salas, a prominent Jewish shipbuilder and merchant, was sitting at his desk immersed in reading. The powerful, bellowing wind that had been blowing for a few hours did not disturb him since he was quite familiar with tropical storms, but that night he paused and looked out of the wide window of his study. There was something uncanny and ominous in the sound, something he had not sensed before while living on the island of Curacao, where he felt more at ease since it was the home of his ancestors for over a hundred years. The darkness of the night was profound, there were no stars to be seen, and the moon was non-existent, yet the dismal bleakness of the night seemed to become even more tenebrous, as if one was sinking into a murky abyss. It began to rain and the sound of the soaking torrent, mingled with the wailing shrill of the wind and crashing thunder, reinforced a sensation of upcoming doom.[1] He got up and stood at the window, trying to shake off his uneasiness. He was a tall and powerfully built man of stern appearance, always meticulously dressed, to whom elegance and faultless manners were a way of life. He was concerned about his ships; some of them were out at sea with their cargo of lumber, fruits and vegetables. They sailed to various islands of the Caribbean and would come back to Cumana filled with guano, bird droppings that served as fertilizer.[2] He liked to deal with merchandise that brought benefit to people. The lumber he sent out was important for the economy of the islands that purchased it, the produce was nourishment for the population, and the guano enriched the earth so that it could provide food for humans. All this had also brought him a very good profit and, as his business grew over the years, he had become quite wealthy.

There followed a display of lightning so powerful that the sky itself seemed to be on fire, but it did not last too long and slowly even the wind seemed to subside. After a while he returned to his desk to continue his work. When he lifted his head once again he thought that he had noticed a flicker of light somewhere in the distance. His house faced the ocean and it was possible that people were rushing to the harbor, looking around with lamps to see how much damage the terrible wind had caused. The masts of the ships there could have been snapped, the anchors torn, and sailors injured. Yet, the light seemed to come from afar, farther in the ocean, not at the shore . . .

He opened a massive mahogany box where he kept his large sea captain's spyglass. He picked up the telescope and, opening the window, adjusted and focused it as much as he could in the direction of the flickering light he had seen. It appeared again but he could not see much beyond it. He summoned a servant and ordered him to call a few of the sailors who worked for him, and commanded them to be prepared to launch several rowboats so that he could go out to sea and check whether there was a ship offshore in need of assistance.

Dressed in his storm gear with a wide hat and leaving behind the ornamental cane that he usually carried, David Haim Salas left his house and, fighting the wind that had not subsided completely, joined his crew at the harbor. The boats had been launched and, getting into one of them, he watched the inhabitants of Cumana struggling on the shore while the boats pulled out of the dock with great difficulty. Some of the natives seemed to be paralyzed with awe and stood motionless, while others, fearful of a repeat of the first stormy outburst, were confused, not knowing what to do first, desperate because of the amount of damage that the hurricane had caused. Many had not yet dared to come out of their dwellings where they had taken refuge at the onset of the storm. Some trees had been ripped out by their roots, many bungalows destroyed, and several people killed or hurt. The mood of the ocean seemed to have changed and the waves, although still enormous, did not rise to spectacular heights anymore as if their strength had been used up. David Haim Salas was a courageous man who trusted in Adonai, the God of his forefathers, and knew that nothing would happen without His will. The remarkable confidence he showed had a deep effect on his servants who felt energized seeing him sitting calmly at the bow of the wildly tossing boat looking into the distance from where a sinking ship had sent its signal for help.

They rowed out of the bay and were able, soon afterwards, to locate a ship that was in deep trouble indeed. The schooner, a two-masted vessel on which the sails were not square rigged, was already half sunk. Under the circumstances, the crew had not been able to maneuver the vessel properly and, despite their desperate attempts to reach shore, the masts were demolished and they all ended up in the water. The rescuers were astounded by the scope of the destruction that the hurricane had wrought in a relatively short amount of time. It had not been a very big ship, as they could see, but was a sleek and strong schooner, a navigating craft that must have performed its seafaring role in the past with great success and had known how to tackle the dangers of the deep seas. Not this time. This was the end of the American Schooner *Cohannit* whose last mission had been doomed. The sailors were drowning and David Haim Salas, together with his men, quickly went to work, pulling them as fast as they could into the rowboats. Many were struggling in the water and trying to fight the treacherous waves so they would not succumb. The rowboats left with as many of the victims as they could hold and quickly returned several times to rescue those who were still hanging on to the rafts of broken wood and pieces of mast that were floating in the ocean. Despite the disaster, the crew of the USS *Cohannit* was extremely fortunate—not even a single man was lost at sea and they were all taken to Salas' mansion. Señor Salas immediately summoned a doctor for those who had been weakened by the ordeal, were near to death, and needed urgent medical care. Those who could handle it on their own were given dry clothes and food, and provided with temporary accommodations. All in all there were forty-seven American sailors and thirteen officers who had been saved that night from the claws of the angry ocean.

David Haim Salas's home was a very large sprawling house, quite unique in Cumana in those days. It was very much like the traditional courtyard dwelling typical of rich Jews who lived in Spain before the Inquisition and from where Salas' family originally came. The atrium—the central open area and core of the house—provided ventilation as well as illumination. It was decorated with a multitude of plants and fountains that helped to ease the heat of the day. It also was used as an ornate reception area and was surrounded by many rooms that served as bedrooms. There was an elaborate dining room and, farther down, there was a smaller courtyard that led to office spaces as well as guest rooms and servant quarters. The rural patio house was introduced to Cumana in the early sixteenth century when the city was the first one to be founded in the Venezuelan Caribbean by the Spaniards.[3] The distribution of the rooms and the overall design of the home were exquisite and luxurious, proper to the wealth and rank of the Salas family.[4] No wonder that the crew of the American Schooner *Cohannit* felt extremely comfortable and blessed to have found such a haven after their terrible ordeal.

While recovering and still unable to believe that they had not perished, the rescued sailors faced the beauty and tranquility of many Caribbean days that often follow the stormy violence of hurricanes of that magnitude. David Haim Salas was a gracious host and, in addition to making sure that all the men were treated like guests, given comfortable shelter, plentiful food, needed medical care, and all necessary clothing, immediately dispatched a message to the United States to notify the authorities, as well as the families of the crew, of what had happened and that all the sailors were safe. The telegraph was an evolving technology then and, despite the fact that there was an attempt to deploy it across the oceans, it was not completely successful until about the late 1800s and early 1900s and, thus, was very slow and faulty at times. Salas arranged for the officers in the party to reach another port in Venezuela from where they could sail to the United States. Only the officers were able to leave and it took about a month for them to get home. Once in Washington, they reported the details of the incident to the government and requested that a vessel be sent to pick up the sailors who had been left behind. It took a long time, about nine months, until a ship arrived and docked at the shore of Cumana and the crew sailed home. Throughout all this time, Salas took care of the sailors' needs and, when they left Cumana, he felt a deep sense of satisfaction that he had done a good deed. It did not occur to him that what he had accomplished was way beyond the kindness and concern any person would show to other human beings.

Not too long after the sailors' departure, Salas received a letter from the secretary of the United States Navy thanking him and asking for a bill so that the government could reimburse him for the expenses he had incurred. He answered, expressing his pleasure at having been able to help but refusing to submit a bill since he had done, as he put it, *"only that which my God required of me."* Being a religious Jew and not just a man with a very big heart, he could not and would not accept any payment for the deed he had done since he believed it had been meant to happen and that he had been destined to take care of it. Some time later a second letter arrived, this time from the secretary of State, sending him once again heartfelt thanks but insisting that the government felt obliged to offer some reimbursement. Salas refused again in his gallant and polite way that was, nevertheless, a stubborn, final statement of his decision not to accept any money for what he had done. A third letter followed. This time the President of The United States, himself, felt the need to write to this very remarkable and generous man and express his gratitude and that of his nation. He did not insist on the reimbursement anymore but rather respectfully inquired as to whether Salas' religion would permit him to accept a personal gift as a token of appreciation. President Rutherford Hayes, the nineteenth president of the United States, a Methodist, had the reputation—very similar to that of Salas'—for being hardworking, methodical, and impeccably honest, and as such it was no wonder that he felt great admiration for the Jewish business man who cherished the same basic values he did. David Haim Salas sent a polite letter of thanks to the president and graciously accepted the offer.

Almost a year later, the United States ambassador to Venezuela paid a formal visit to Salas and presented him with a marvelous gift. The president had commissioned Tiffany to design a silver sterling bowl, especially for David Haim Salas. The magnificent vessel has engravings on two sides that retell the story of the American Schooner *Cohannit*. It depicts the sinking ship with the rowboats coming to its rescue and the American flag flying upside down, which is an international sign of distress. The other side of the silver bowl shows the crossed flags of both the United States and Venezuela, the top of the rim is ringed with a series of naval anchors and tridents, and the lower base is surrounded by beautiful dolphins. The bowl sits on an impressive solid black, ebony turned base with a silver plaque, which has the following words engraved upon it: "Presented by the President of The United States of America to Senor Don David Haim Salas in recognition of his Heroism, Humanity and Generosity in rescuing and subsisting the crew of the American Schooner "Cohannit" wrecked near Cumana, Venezuela, 1877". Salas received the ambassador in his study, accepted the wonderful present with grace, and felt honored by it as well as the presence of the distinguished visitor. When he left, Salas looked once again at the shiny bowl. It had been placed on his desk, the afternoon's intense light penetrated through the window and made it shimmer and glitter so that it looked almost as if, at any moment, its sparkle could create a fire. David Haim Salas smiled with a deep sense of contentment and, feeling blessed, suddenly recalled the saying from the Talmud: *"Cling steadfastly to that which is good."*

Source Note

Based on an interview in April 2003 with David Haim Salas' great-grandson, Hugo de Castro Salas, a lawyer who resides in Encino, CA. David Haim Salas was a thirty-four-year-old bachelor at the time of the *Cohannit* rescue. Later he married in Curacao into a well-known Caribbean family whose name was Abinum de Lima. He had ten children, the eldest of whom was Dr. Moises Haim Salas, the grandfather of Hugo de Castro Salas and one of the first ophthalmologists in Latin America. The bowl is now proudly owned by Mr. Hugo de Castro Salas and treasured by the family's many descendants.

Text Notes

1. The storm described here that hit Cumana was most probably the one on October 3–4, 1877, when a hurricane was spotted in the eastern Caribbean Sea, and the island of Curacao (located opposite and very close to the Venezuelan shore) was devastated (*http://www.hpc.ncep.noaa.gov/research/roth/valaterphur.htm*).

2. Guano deposits are dried bird droppings, which are used as fertilizer. Ancient civilizations in Peru and Central America used it for farming as early as 100 B.C.E. to increase the size of their harvest. The name guano derives from *guanay*, the native name given to black cormorants that are found on many islands along the Humboldt Current and are the main producers of guano. Guano contains nitrogen that helps the soil become rich and fertile. The sea bird guano business was first begun on Navassa Island in 1857, which is a two-square mile United States territory located in the Caribbean Sea between Jamaica and Haiti.

3. Cumana—The town was the first to be founded by the Spanish in the American Continent in 1551 under the command of Gonzalo de Campo. Its name in the native language means: the union between the sea and the river. It is also where one of the most important Venezuelans was born—Antonio Jose de Sucre, who fought for the independence of South America and liberated it from Spain.

4. Courtyard house, history of: Gasparini Graziano, *La arquitectura colonial en Venezuela* (Caracas: Armitano, 1985).

A Dream Come True

THE IQUITOS STORY

The choir was very powerful. The sound vibrated and echoed throughout the whole area, sending waves of diverse chirping melodies far and wide. It was loud but consistent and as such, although tedious, it became a part of the landscape, an invisible scenery that blended with it all. If visible, one could have seen a variety of unbelievable birds of multicolored feathers that live and die, high up in the Andes of Peru, around the lake Quistococha, in the outskirts of the town of Iquitos. There would be the blackish Sierra finch with its bright golden rump, the yellow-faced, attractive tiny parrot Maranon, white-chinned Thistletails, playful and very loud torrent ducks, some black-billed thrushes that tend to sing their hearts out, and many spectacular green and white hummingbirds. Many species of birds are very vocal but hard to see; either they are small like some owls or, even the bigger ones, blend into the vegetation despite their bright colors. That particular day, the symphony was very powerful, as if the bird population knew that a special ceremony was being performed and they wanted to participate in the festivities. It was just a pity there was no conductor and thus, at times, the music became somewhat overbearing since each bird was singing randomly at his or her own pace.

In the waters of the placid *laguna*, not too far from the shore, there stood a group of bare-chested men and children while, in the distance, not too far away, stood a handful of modestly clad women. They were not there to swim or play despite the fact that it was a hot day in early August and the humidity was high. Their symbolic submersion into the waters of the lake was a part of the final stage of their conversion into Judaism. They were all natives of Iquitos and the descendants of the settlers in that region of the northern part of the Peruvian jungle. They do not know much about their predecessors but consider themselves the children of a small group of people, most probably Marranos, that settled down in that area during the colonial times when there were many clans and small tribes that lived on the various slopes of the Andes. Despite the fact that their ancestors were baptized, they inherited certain traditions and customs which they had held sacred for centuries and which in the end brought them back to the ancient faith of their forefathers. These are the Jewish Iquitenos, the Judios Charapas, or Jewish Mestizos whose story can never be forgotten. These people have no quarrel or problems of identity with Jewish communities in Peru, the rest of Latin America, or other places in the world; they are just anxious to belong to Am Adonai, the Hebrew nation as a whole and the land of Israel. Their devotion is as intense as their willingness to do whatever necessary, to be once again what they believe they have always been—Jews.

Although many small clans lived in this northern part of Peruvian jungle—in the department of Loreto—in ancient times, the city of Iquitos, which is its capital, was founded only in 1864. During the Colonial period the Spanish founded towns and created a network of routes that enabled the tribes to communicate and trade. Toward the end of the nineteenth century, Iquitos became famous thanks to the rubber industry. This lasted for about twenty-five years and enabled a big development in that region. One can see the remains of the past splendor and opulence in the old colonial mansions that still stand along the riverbanks. The story goes that around 1905 a group of young Jews in their early twenties came from different places in search of their fortune. Some remained in the Peruvian jungle, some advanced inland, and some found their way to the coast. Those who stayed worked in whatever was available, many of them were very poor merchants that had to cope with life in the jungle which was tremendously harsh. In a way, it is a miracle that over the years they were able to keep their traditions; nobody told them how to go about it or how to cherish their faith. No Jewish girls could be found in that area so they married local females and continued to live their very solitary and secluded life. In time many habits were forgotten, certain rituals were not performed anymore, and some of their descendants wore the cross as well as the Magen David, displaying both of them in good faith without knowing why. Nevertheless, most burials were performed according to Jewish customs, and women were very meticulous, in particular, about their monthly cleanliness routine and participated in ritual baths. Being extremely poor they turned their dresses inside out on special occasions, such as the Shabbat, so as to feel more festive.

The Judios Charapas displayed pride also in the Indian culture that they had adopted. The art they learned, the skill of weaving and knowledge of materials, were exceptional abilities that enabled them to make a better living. They ate typical Loreto dishes such as *motelo* (turtle meat soup) or *juanes* (tamales filled with beef) as well as *palometa* (fish soup) and even *cecina* (dried and smoked pork). Some of them were aware that they should not mix the meat with milk products and so, while eating these dishes, they abstained, for example, from the tasty *papa ala Huancaina* (a typical potato cheese soup) and *platano frito* (plantain banana fried and dipped in sweet milk sauce). They drank traditional Inca drinks, fermented or not. They even made a habit of consuming the legendary "siete raices" (seven roots) medicinal tonic liqueur which is taken on a daily basis by many Amazonians to enhance their health and well-being. Basically they viewed Judaism not necessarily as a race and religion, but more as ancestry and lineage of which they were proud, and rules were not, necessarily, always applicable. As many Amazonians they also respected nature and took it for granted to live in harmony with the forces that govern it. They have always been blessed (or maybe at times cursed) with a very vivid imagination that is another characteristic of the people of the Amazon. They were in contact with the magical and spiritual context of the jungle that a person living in that area cannot ignore. The shamans or the *curanderos* were always revered teachers of the unknown. The mystical and ancient relationships with nature were practiced and in time there came into being a revealing interaction between the shamanic knowledge and modern science that the *mestizos* were aware of as well.

Things have, nevertheless, changed in the last ten years since the tribunal of the rabbis, comprised of Rabbi Guillermo Bronstein, Rabbi

Claudio Kupchik, and Rabbi Alex Felch, has helped the Judios Charapas step back into the covenant of Judaism. These three very special individuals taught them the sacred book of the Torah, explained to them the intricacies of the Jewish law, fortified their spirit as human beings, and gave them new purpose in their lives. Brit Milah was performed on all the males and all other required rituals were followed carefully and meticulously. The three rabbis helped the "newly born" Jews of Iquitos to overcome the obstacles and many difficulties they encountered while performing their unusual task. On August 5, 2002, while being submerged in the calm waters of the laguna, a natural Mikveh, the Judios Charapas reached the culmination of their dream. Finally, the road that spread out in front of them led from the dense and intricate jungle of the Amazon to the eternal city of Jerusalem, back to their roots.

That night, the sky was exceptionally brilliant. Shining, twinkling stars seemed very close, within a hand's reach, a marvelous sight to behold and relish only in the depths of the Amazon. The small huts and adobes of the residents were engulfed in the glittering moonlight that shed its magic on the luxurious landscape. No hotel or palace in the world could boast with a larger number of stars to indicate its excellence. In this forlorn little place, in the navel of the earth, people enjoyed the best accommodations anyone could ever wish for.

Source note

Based mainly on a video (Iquitos, Peru, August 2002) provided by Rabbi Guillermo Bronstein and on some of my Peruvian interviews in August 2001. Ariel Segal's book, *Jews of the Amazon Self Exile in Paradise*, The Jewish Publication Society, Philadelphia, 1999, is a detailed study of the life of Jews in the Peruvian Amazon.

Seeking Wisdom

$\mathcal{M}$any years ago, when the forests south of the river Bio-Bio were still impenetrable, there lived in the beautiful lake district of Chile a very poor family. The father and mother had two children, a girl and a boy, who helped them to fish in the lakes and gather pine nuts in the woods, and thus they had a very simple yet happy existence. The emerald green forests, the white-capped mountains seen from afar, and the bubbling waterfalls were home to the children who spent a lot of their time playing and wandering around. They enjoyed the balmy summers and spent the rainy and cold winters in their hut, which provided them good shelter when they needed it. As time went by, Araceli and Theodo, who had never learned to read or write, started asking questions and wondering about many things for which neither the parents nor neighbors had any explanations. They were very bright children; Araceli, who was the older one, pondered why certain things were right or wrong, and Theodo was curious to find out what was behind the smoking, snow-covered volcanoes he saw from his hut. The children had heard from a wandering, old Mapuche Indian, who had spent a stormy night in their house, that on a mountain peak far away there lived an old, wise man that had the answers to any and all questions. Thus, one day, with their parents' permission, Araceli and Theodo left their home and started a pilgrimage to the top of the mysterious volcano in search of knowledge.

It was summer time and the children took with them some food and a few blankets to protect them from the cold weather in the mountains. They tied their bundle on top of Pancha, their favorite llama. Pancha was a beautiful, young alpaca; her wool was white with shades of gray and she carried herself with great dignity. She was sure-footed ascending hills on any kind of terrain and exceptionally gentle and communicative. Araceli and Theodo were her best friends and they understood her humming when she was content and also knew to expect danger when she emitted short, shrill sounds. She was a priceless companion on any trip and they felt more secure taking her with them on their adventure.

They walked for many days and saw marvelous landscapes. One night they camped at the shores of a beautiful lake that had unusually light green water and from where they could see three volcanoes that seemed to come closer the more they looked at them. Araceli washed her long, dark hair and enjoyed looking at her image in the tranquil waters that reflected the tall trees that grew around it. They were familiar with some of the trees such as the Araucarias, and they also noticed many unusual, tall reeds that Pancha was particularly interested in tasting. Araceli was delighted when Theodo found in that dense vegetation a large pinkish flower that blooms only once every twenty-five years. The children felt that it was a good omen since those flowers are so rare and they noticed the bloom just in time to prevent Pancha from eating it. That night they slept very peacefully and gathered strength, which they needed for the arduous ascent to the top of the volcano.

After a few days the children encountered different scenery; the hills became steeper and the soil very rocky. There were hardly any trees or shrubs to be seen and no animals, small or large. They still had quite a bit of pine nuts to keep them from being hungry, grass for Pancha, and water to quench their thirst. However, the winds began picking up as if hundreds of people were hissing and whistling, and it was difficult to breathe. They slept cuddled behind a rock and holding on to Pancha, who did not seem to be very uncomfortable. The next day they continued crawling along some cliffs, battling the wind, and, from afar, saw an imposing peak that fitted the description the traveling Indian had given them. They were heartened to be close to their destination but felt very cold, hungry, and thirsty, since their water had frozen during the night. Pancha was covered with a layer of frost and there were even icicles hanging from the strands of her long coat of wool. She seemed tired and kept spitting over and over again, since the remnants of the icy grass that she had eaten did not appeal to her at all. Yet, no matter what, it never occurred to the children to even consider turning back before reaching the old man on top of the mountain.

Finally they saw the lip of the crater. They wondered where the old wise man could be living and just hoped that he had a little hut tucked away somewhere where they could warm up and have something to drink before talking to him. As they approached the tip of the peak, the strong winds died down and, climbing with great effort, they reached the top of the volcano. From the edge of the crater they looked down and saw a lake of hot red lava and shivered as they noticed some stones continually hurling down into the menacing depth of the pit. And then they saw it—a few steps leading down to a small shack glued to the slope of the crater with a large window to its side and a narrow door in front of it.

The door opened and at the threshold stood a small, old man dressed in a white robe, a tiny cap on his head, and a golden shawl with fringes around his shoulders. He motioned to them to approach and without saying a word, as if he had been expecting them, led them into his hut. As bleak as it looked from the outside, it was close to a palace inside. The walls were whitewashed and emitted warmth. A large table was covered with food and steaming drinks, far beyond anything the freezing, half-starved children had hoped for. Pancha stopped spitting as soon as she got in, her conical ears stood up rigidly, and she hummed happily seeing that some better food was awaiting her. The old man asked the children to be seated and served a wonderful meal of delightful foods they had never eaten before. Soon they were well fed and felt comfortable sitting on rounded warm rocks that seemed to be softer than any chair they had ever used. They did not even remember when they fell asleep but woke up the next morning refreshed, happy, and very grateful to the old man for his heartfelt hospitality.

The time had come to ask him all they wanted to know. The old man smiled at them affectionately and told them that in addition to his name—which was Emmanuel—he could not tell them much but give them an answer to only one question. Araceli felt disappointed and quite devastated, since she had so many questions, and looked at Theodo as if asking for help. However, Theodo by now knew what the top of the mountain held and was not really interested in asking anything else in particular. He sat on a rock, petting Pancha on the neck, and was quite anxious to start their journey back home. Araceli came closer to the old man and finally asked him the one question that was most important to her: "What is truth?"

He smiled a broad smile and said, "Cuando como, como; cuando duermo, duermo . . ." meaning, "When I eat, I eat; when I sleep, I sleep . . ."[1] He then gave them a bundle full of food to help them on their way back and led them to the door. They thanked him many times and stepped out into the cold. Theodo and Pancha were in a rush to get off the volcano and did not look back; but Araceli did and when she turned to wave her last goodbye, she did not see the little hut nor the old man anymore—they were all gone—the only thing that remained was the sheer rock on the side of the mountain . . .

Source Note

Based on an interview with Adriana Balter in Santiago, Chile, March 2002. Adriana heard this story from her mother, Tosca Balter, who is the author of a wonderful collection of tales: *Espejos y otros Cuentos*, Zeta editores, Santiago, 1997. At times, Adriana's mother would modify certain elements in the story to make it longer when her children could not fall asleep or to make it more interesting.

Text Note

1. The answer given by the old man, who is dressed as a rabbi and has a Biblical name, is puzzling; yet it basically conveys the message that things inexorably come and go in a certain order. At any rate, it gives children and young people something to ponder about and that could be the aim of the tale . . .

The Lost One

$\mathcal{D}$aniel Nachmias had never felt so fearful, and at the same time elated, as on the day he first left the town of Belém and penetrated into the jungle hoping to make a fortune in rubber tapping.[1] He had arrived in Brazil after a long and tiring voyage from Morocco and had stayed for a while with a relative who was his only connection in the New World. This second cousin had made it possible for him to travel to Belém since his parents had been too poor to send him on any trips to faraway places.[2] When he left, he had promised them and his only sister that he would accumulate wealth and return or send for them to join him. It was quite common for young Moroccan Jews, in the middle of the nineteenth century, to flee depressed economic conditions in Morocco and search for a better life in South America, particularly in the Amazonia.

The relative provided Daniel with a supply of food and took him by canoe a few miles up the river Para. He left him at a place along the river-bank where access to the jungle was easy and where he was sure to meet other people who made their living extracting latex from the rubber trees. When Daniel saw the canoe departing and his relative waving goodbye and growing smaller and smaller in the distance, he felt apprehensive, yet he touched his backpack where he had put the prayer book his mother had given him and felt reinforced and hopeful. It was hot and clammy, the humidity was very high, and it started raining. He pulled his hat closer to his forehead and stepped into the forest, praying for good luck.

The Amazon reached out and engulfed his senses. Sheets of rain were pounding the forest but under the heavy foliage Daniel did not feel it as much and, standing for a while under a thick canopy of an exotic tree he had never seen before, was not uncomfortable. He walked for a couple of hours in the direction he had been instructed and became worried that, contrary to what he had been told, there were no people around at all. He had expected to find rubber tappers along the trail. When night fell, he climbed up a massive tree with widespread branches where he could nestle down and sleep for a few hours. The sounds of the jungle were nerve-wracking to him. He had seen during the day large tropical birds and lots of different kinds of monkeys and flying insects. He was grateful he had boots to protect him from whatever was crawling on the ground, creatures he did not see but had felt and heard earlier while he was hiking. During the long hours of the tropical night his uneasiness mounted, as he had not expected to spend it all by himself but with a group of rubber tappers. The forest grew very dim and there were no rays of sunshine streaming through the tall trees as it had been during the day. It became very dark and noisy and Daniel tried not to imagine the many creatures to which the forest serves as refuge.

When day broke, he continued his walk using his compass pointing north to where the rubber tappers' camp was supposed to be. The diversity of life in the Amazon was startling to him. He had never seen such big, brilliant flowers and the size of some of the giant leaves on the trees and bushes he encountered amazed him. He was not so thrilled, however, to see the huge spiders and snakes that abounded and the many monkeys of different sizes and shapes that jumped in front of him and hung from the branches of the trees. The day passed rather rapidly and another dark night descended on him before he realized it. He started to panic and, trying to calm himself, made up his mind to retrace his steps in the morning unless he could locate the elusive tappers. The next morning, feeling weak and desperate, he was not able to find the trail that would have taken him back. After three days of wandering in the jungle, running out of food supplies, and sleeping in the trees, he thought he was lost forever and doomed to die. He opened his book of prayers and thinking of his family, his old parents and his sister, to whom he had promised better times and instead brought disaster, implored God to save him. That night Daniel felt sick and developed a fever, the haze of humidity hung over him, his eyesight became b l u r r y, and the sweat dripped profusely from his body. He became disoriented and his mind began to wander. He thought that some strange monkeys had lifted him from where he was lying and taken him to a hut where they put him down and washed his body with some tepid water. He was fed a thick liquid that tasted like chocolate and saw the monkeys dancing in a circle, making strange sounds. After that everything was lost in darkness and when he emerged, as if from a hollow pit, he found himself in an Indian village in the middle of the jungle.

It took Daniel a long time to recover from the inevitable fatigue and the weariness that followed his disease. When he regained his strength he realized that he was in the depths of the forest, far away from anybody who could understand him and with no idea how much time had passed since he had fallen ill. Nevertheless, he had been very fortunate that two hunters, from the Kayapo Indian tribe that live in different parts of the Amazon basin, had found him half dead under a tree and taken him to their village where they saved his life.[3] As the days went by he learned to communicate with the Indians who were very compassionate and tended to his needs. Fascinated, he watched them perform ceremonies that included mostly dances within a circle, wearing masks that resembled the faces of monkeys. Later on he found out that the name Kayapo, which means "resembling monkeys", was given to them by neighboring tribes.

The Indians let him help them with their work; he gathered Brazil nuts, which were plentiful in the pristine forest, and learned to extract juice from the Acai palm found in the Amazon and which the Indians believed to have medicinal value. He grew very fond of the chocolate *cupuacu* fruit as well as the tart *camu-camu*, munched *guarana* berries that made him feel energetic, and joined his hosts during their meals.[4] He ate their fish dishes but never touched the meat they brought back from their hunts. He played with the children and learned to paint their faces in many colorful patterns just as their mothers did, but never agreed to be made up by them. Daniel did not fret anymore when he saw large beetles, huge spiders, and enormous blue centipedes crawling around and when the gigantic *cururu* frogs made a racket at night croaking their hearts out. He watched the Indians pointing to the place that the green anacondas frequented and knew how to spot and avoid them. Marveling at the length and size of the formidable snakes, he did not feel anymore like Daniel in the Lion's den fearing the unknown, his faith in God became stronger, and, during sleepless nights, he even believed he might see his family again. He liked to watch the bright toucans and macaws while painting the children's faces with similar shimmering colors. One day, they brought him a gift; he could not believe his eyes; it was the tiniest monkey he had ever seen, not much longer than his forefinger. The Indians had them as pets but also used to place them on their heads since they were very good at catching lice. The littlest creature became Daniel's inseparable companion, never to leave him again.

The days went by, each resembling the other; the seasons seemed not to change, afternoon downpours were the order of the day and then it would be sunny, hot, and humid. He had prayed fervently every single day during his recovery and soon was able to memorize most of the prayers in the book. It comforted him to think that even if he lost it, his memory would serve him well and he would never forget what he cherished more than anything else in the world. The Indians watched him attentively when he prayed. Since he could not find his kippa and covered his head with a big leaf from an adjacent tree, they did the same. They even imitated his motions, not to mock him, but rather as a sign of solidarity. One day he found a tiny colorful woven basket that resembled a yarmulke; he took it into his hut and used it instead of the leaf to cover his head. A thin blanket made out of some weeds served him as a prayer shawl. He tried to calculate how much time had elapsed since he came to the jungle, as he wanted to observe the Jewish holidays. He came to the conclusion that Yom Kippur was approaching and decided to fast and pray as he had done at home. It had always been the most solemn and sacred of all days and he did not want to miss it. When the day came, the Indians became concerned as he refused to eat, but he was able to explain to them, mainly using sign language, that it was a ritual for him, just as the ceremonies they performed. That evening, at dusk, renewed and cleansed, he felt hopeful that he would eventually find a way out of his predicament.

A few days later, while gathering some barks and roots in the forest, he heard voices that were not those of his Indian friends. He rushed through the thicket around him and found himself face to face with the very people he had failed to meet the first day he had stepped into the jungle. It was a group of rubber tappers making their way through the forest with the lumps of latex they had harvested. He told them in his poor Portuguese what had happened to him and they offered to take him with them on their way back to Belém. He gratefully accepted their help and bid goodbye to his Indian friends who had heard the commotion and come to see what was happening. They were not people who showed their emotions but it was obvious they were sorry to see him go. They held him in high regard and assumed that he was some sort of a shaman from another world who had brought them good luck. Daniel thanked them fullheartedly and, holding his prayer book in his hand, his loyal little monkey on his shoulder, and his eyes filled with tears, left his benefactors without looking back.

Five days later he arrived at his relative's house. Daniel told him all about his adventures and proudly pointed out that he had, despite his misfortune, observed Yom Kippur faithfully. The puzzled look on his relative's face made him uneasy. It turned out that having been isolated in the jungle for a long time, he had miscalculated badly and celebrated Yom Kippur on the first day of Passover. Daniel turned pale and felt desolate and forlorn. His cousin, on the other hand, smiled broadly and, hugging him affectionately, reassured him that the intention was what counted and that he had no doubts that Daniel's deep conviction had brought him back safe and sound.[5] He promised him that next time he would have him join a group of tappers before they left for the jungle. Daniel, however, had lost his interest in the rubber industry; he did not want to go back to the forest no matter how profitable it could be; he just wanted to stay in Belém and help his relative in his business, if he would allow him.

And so it came to pass. In time Daniel became a well-to-do partner in the umbrella and glove business his relative owned. It had been introduced into Brazil by Jews, and the natives, who initially had no idea as to the utility of such items, took a fancy to them because of their practical as well as ornamental use.[6] Daniel never became extremely rich, as he had hoped initially, but was able to keep his promise to his family and bring them to Belém. His belief in God deepened, he became very religious, and a benefactor to many in need. His faithful little monkey, whom he affectionately named Kayapo, lived for many years along his side and always slept in a small, red velvet glove placed next to Daniel's bed.

Source Note
Based on an interview with Laura Semo Rosen in Sao Paulo, March 2002.

Text Notes
1. Rubber tapping is a traditional Amazonian activity that does not endanger the forest, as it is not necessary to cut down the trees to extract the latex used in producing the rubber.

2. Belém, in Pará state, one of Brazil's busiest ports, is about 60 miles upriver from the Atlantic Ocean. The river is the Pará, part of the greater Amazon River system, separated from the larger part of the Amazon delta by Ilha de Marajó or Island of Marajó. Belém is comprised of a number of small islands intersected by channels and other rivers. Founded in 1616, Belém was the first European colony on the Amazon but did not become part of the Brazilian nation until 1775. As the gateway to the Amazon, the port and city grew tremendously in size and importance during the nineteenth century rubber boom.

3. The Kayapo Indians live in the tropical rainforests of Brazil. Circles are one of the tribe's symbols since they worship the sun and the moon and their circular orbits. They paint their bodies with different patterns representing their status in society. Men paint their own bodies and faces; so do the women who also make up their children and reapply the paints very often. Several varieties of fish are their main sources of food as they are so plentiful in their rivers. They still hunt and fish mostly with bows and arrows, although they have learned some modern ways from the white man.

4. Guarana is a berry that grows in northern Brazil and Venezuela. Its name is derived from the Guarani tribe that lives in the Amazon. They believe it has magical qualities and helps cure some illnesses. The main ingredient in Guarana is similar to caffeine and that is the reason for the energy boost people get from it. The Guarana–based drink is very common and popular in Brazil (tastes somewhat similar to 7-Up) but difficult to find in most other South American countries.

5. The observance of a sacred day—*When Passover became Yom Kippur*—The singular effort of Daniel to follow a certain very important religious code was really all that mattered. Rabbis have pointed out many times that it is mainly the intention that counts regardless of the time a certain deed is performed. Daniel's religious belief and his deep devotion were much more intense than that of a regular Jew observing Yom Kippur on the right day. Just like the rabbi's under-

taking in Y.L. Peretz' s famous story "If Not Higher Than That," Daniel's prayers, in his case, had more impact than if he had followed the regular pattern.

6. The Jews of Brazil and Brazilian culture – Comments by Diane Kuperman, a writer and reporter of Egyptian origin, who specializes in anti-Semitism and organizes conferences on Folklore and Ethnology—Rio de Janeiro, March 2002. The Jews have been influenced by Brazilian culture, but have also had an impact on the native population in more than one way. They not only introduced new items, such as umbrellas and gloves, which the people had never seen before and which became very popular and useful, but also some of their mannerisms, sayings, and expressions penetrated into the general culture. This, no doubt, brought also some alienation at times since anything unknown creates fear and objection in a new society. Fleeing the horrors of the Inquisition, initially at least, Jews did not proclaim their origin openly and just wanted to become a part of the general community. The studies of ethnology and folklore have become a growing trend in Brazilian culture, and the Jewish traditions, mainly the Sephardic and Oriental, are proving to be very important.

In Between the Snowflakes

It was a gray and freezing day in January of 1945, the twelfth day of January to be exact, a day Marita will remember as long as she lives. In her mind's calendar, it is circled in red forever after. Marita was, at that time, a young girl living in Nazi occupied Budapest. She had been born Jewish but—because of certain circumstances in her mother's life, who had become Catholic and married a Christian—was unaware of it until that fateful month. The intense disputes between the Orthodox Jews on the one hand and those advocating integration and assimilation on the other deeply affected Marita's mother, just as it did the lives of many Jews in Hungary and other East European countries. The violent opposition from the religious sector did not prevent people from rebelling and mixed marriages were not uncommon. This factor also helped many to escape, at least temporarily, from the nightmares of anti-Semitism, which flourished in Hungary in the years before the war and became more dominant towards the end of the Nazi era.

In the autumn of 1944, close to the end of World War II, the Germans occupied Hungary in order to fight the Russians who were very near the borders. At the same time, Ferenc Szalasi became head of state in Hungary and replaced Miklos Horthy, who had tried but failed to negotiate a secret armistice for his country with the western Allies. Szalasi, an erratic, radical ex-army officer, the leader of the Hungarian fascist Arrow Cross party, had advocated a pro-Nazi policy since 1937 and was extremely anti-Semitic. The Jews that lived in the provinces were the first to be deported to the death camps, mainly to Auschwitz. Thousands of them were also sent to the Austrian border to dig fortification trenches, and hundreds died on the way before reaching the destination. Initially, many were able to evade expulsion by hiding in the capital or in ghettos outside the city. The deportation and confinement to ghettos were not condemned by most of the public since they felt little sympathy for the Jews and their willingness to help the victims was minimal. After the deportation from the provinces was completed, Szalasi ordered the half-a-million Jews in Budapest to be concentrated in about two thousand houses that were marked for that purpose with yellow stars. A curfew had to be observed by them and they lived in utter despair and destitution waiting for their deportation. This was the last stage in Szalasi's plan of completing the *Entjudung*—"ridding of the Jews"— following the ideal of Adolf Hitler's "final solution."

Marita lived in one of Budapest's suburbs with her mother and stepfather. She did not remember her own father who had died when she was just two years old, and her mother had married a man who was also a convert to the Christian religion. Her mother and stepfather tried to keep her life as normal as possible and took her every Sunday to a local church for the services. She did not know at that time that her maternal grandparents had belonged to a synagogue that was not far from the church and that they had been devastated by their daughter's decision to leave their faith. Marita felt bewildered and uncertain when she found out that she was Jewish. She realized suddenly that she belonged to the "dirty race" and did not know how to handle it.

Her uncle, her mother's brother, was a member of the Partisans that fought the Nazis and their Hungarian allies. He knew the city as the palm of his hand and was not seen or heard for days and weeks at times because of the danger involved in his missions. He was well informed about the movements of the German and Hungarian armies and knew some of the secret plans of Szalasi before they were carried out. One evening that fateful autumn when Jews were being deported and hurled into ghettoes, he appeared suddenly and told them that it was imperative for the whole family to leave the house at once and find shelter somewhere else since that particular street was due for deportation the next morning. He had already arranged a place for them to hide, not all together but in separate homes of people who would help them. Within a couple of hours they collected a few of their most precious and essential things and snuck out into the dead of night. They left behind most of their belongings and ran. Marita was taken in and hidden by a Catholic woman named Rozika, the sister of her uncle's ex-wife. Rozika lived in a lower class neighborhood, in an old, weather worn three-story building. Her small, very modest apartment consisted of a simple kitchen, a bathroom, and a narrow corridor that led to a bedroom. It was just like all the other flats in the complex; they were almost identical on all the floors.

Rozika was extremely kind to Marita, did all she could to make her feel comfortable, and tried to hide from the child the deadly danger she was in. Marita found out a few days after she arrived in Rozika's home that her maternal grandfather was also staying in the building but she was warned not to address him or even hint at the fact that she knew who he was. She had been reprimanded severely after greeting him in the corridor the first time she saw him descending the stairs from the upper floors. Marita's mother was in another part of town and so were other relatives. The uncle considered it safer to disperse them as much as possible and, in any case, did not have much of a choice in the matter. People were extremely apprehensive and even the brave ones among them willing to take at the most only one refugee. They all knew that they were playing with death.

On that cold and gloomy January 12, early in the morning, Marita heard heavy and repeated knocks on the wooden gate outside the house. A group of Hungarian Nazi soldiers were pounding on the door since they had been informed that there were some Jews in the building and had come to flush them out of their hiding place. Marita became extremely frightened despite the fact that she had in her pocket a birth certificate stating that she was Catholic, born to a Christian father. She had been sleeping with the papers for days and quickly tried to flatten a couple of corners that had bent without her realizing it. The soldiers pushed the door open and ordered all the tenants to gather outside. They stood in the small yard that was covered with snow in freezing temperatures. Some of the people who had not had time to dress and not been allowed to take their coats looked like specters in their thin garments; their skin quickly acquired a bluish tint and their teeth began to chatter. They all moved silently as the soldiers screamed at them to stand in line while at the same time one could hear the roar of the allies' planes that were dropping bombs all over the city. Marita's Aunt Rozika was not standing next to her since she had been late getting out of the house; she had been so nervous that she could not find her own papers; for a few minutes she had been unable to move, unable to find anything at all. The soldiers prevented her from joining Marita, and so she waved and smiled at the girl from afar, trying to reassure her, without being able to say a word, that things would be all right. Marita saw her grandfather, dressed as a simple peasant, standing at the end of the line behind some religious Jews who would not disguise themselves and insisted on wearing their kaftans and typical hats. They had obviously signed their own death sentences. A dog belonging to one of the tenants was barking like it was demented and would not stop. One of the soldiers, without giving it much thought, lifted his rifle and shot the poor creature in the head. It collapsed but did not die right away. Its heartbreaking moans filled the small yard with a horrible wailing sound that seemed, for a few seconds, to overwhelm the shrill screams and orders of the soldiers and the booming noise of the menacing planes.

All of a sudden, a solemn silence descended on them. The planes seemed to have disappeared from the sky, the dog had died, and the soldiers had finished lining up the people and demanded to see their papers. Marita had been so horrified staring at the animal's body shaking in its last moments of agony, watching the crimson stain that had spread all around it in the white snow, that for a few moments she had not been aware of anything else. A soldier pushed her angrily with the rifle and she could barely answer his questions. She showed him her papers without daring to lift her eyes and told him, as she had been instructed to say, that her father was dead and her mother lived in another town as they had been separated by the war. Marita saw his huge, black, shining boots in front of her, observed her own distorted face reflected in their polish, and believed, at that very moment, that they were the boots of a horrendous ogre who had come to devour her. She was trembling and the officer repeated his question. This time she whispered hoarsely that her mother was dead and that her father lived in another town. She was confused and terrified, and did not even know what she was saying, but the soldier took it as sign that she was lying and a Jewess at that. She was very tiny and frail, the short black hair glued frozen to her head, and her dark eyes filled with glittering tears as she finally looked up at the man who was not a giant, as she had imagined, but small, short, and quite ordinary. However, he was the judge, passed the verdict, and told her to stand next to the fence with the other Jews. Her aunt was also pushed to the wall since she had helped a Jew and thus was doomed to the same fate. Rozika was kneeling in the wet, soft snow, holding on to her rosary and praying. She told Marita to do the same. They were both sure they were going to die, that only a few minutes were left before they would be exterminated just the way the dog had been.

At that very exact moment a plane flew over their heads and dropped a bomb. There was a ghastly, thundering noise, since it was a close hit, and pieces of wood, crumbling plaster, and clusters of wall and glass were flying all over the place. Heavy, brown, dense debris engulfed the yard. Marita was in a complete daze; she thought she was already dead; she could not see much, could not hear anything; life seemed to have stopped and disintegrated . . . later she found out that there were many wounded and that one woman had been killed. But— at the moment when it happened—she did not sense anything except that somebody grabbed her arm and literally dragged her inside the house, into the kitchen, opened the cupboard, and shoved her in, pushing her behind some dishes, baskets, and paper bags. As small as she was, when she came to herself, she could barely sit all folded up and even breathing became a chore. It had been Rozika's mother who had pulled her out of a pile of rubble and literally carried her and placed her on the bottom of the cupboard. She warned her not to make a sound or move an inch until she came back to fetch her.

Marita stayed in the dark closet for many hours. She saw, through the cracks in the old cupboard door, the light change as dusk settled in and never, ever again did she feel the kind of terror she had experienced that day. She did not sense any hunger or thirst, and does not remember whether she managed to control her bodily needs while confined in the cupboard. It was winter and, as a blessing from the heavens, dark- ness fell early. The confusion and chaos outside had subsided and the soldiers, who seemed to be unharmed, collected the people they could find and pushed them into the waiting trucks. Many had taken advantage of the situation and escaped. Rozika had done the same and disappeared somewhere in the house.

The soldiers did not give up though; they were talking and pointing at the upper floors of the building as if they intended to go there in search of more victims. The manager of the house, who was a kind man, remembered that he had a bottle of *palinka*—a favorite alcoholic beverage of the Hungarians, made mostly of ripe apricots—in the kitchen and cleverly decided to use it in order to save some of the people who had not yet been found. He invited the soldiers into his bedroom where there was a sofa and, playing a good-hearted fool, asked them to drink with him to celebrate the fact that they had not been killed by the air raid. The soldiers obliged and drank heartily, laughing and making abusive comments and obscene jokes about the Jews they had found. The bottle of palinka was emptied pretty soon but it was not enough to stupefy the soldiers to the extent that they would give up their search. Fortunately, they did not find any more victims and after a while departed half drunk, leaving the manager with a stern warning to notify them if he found any hiding Jews or else he too would share their fate.

There lived in the building a young boy who was somewhat retarded. He worked as a servant, did the cleaning chores and errands, and it was he who came, after those long and dreadful hours, to fetch Marita and pull her out of her hiding place. She had difficulty standing and walking for a while and felt somewhat dizzy, but the boy did not give her much time to recover and pushed her out into the yard that was by then empty. It was snowing lightly and almost pitch-dark but Marita could see, close to the fence, a body covered with newspapers. It was that of the woman who had been killed during the air raid. She felt desperation and fear engulfing her again and before she had any time to absorb what she was seeing, the young boy pushed her down into the snow and, as a joke, covered her with two pieces of newspaper that he had removed from the corpse. He thought it was amusing to pretend that Marita was also dead. When she rose with difficulty she caught a glimpse of the deceased woman's face, her eyes open and glassy, her mouth stretched in a grimace of horror, one of her hands stiff, frozen, and pointing upwards toward the sky. As weak as she was, Marita ran as if her life depended on it to the entrance of the cellar where people hid during the bombings and where they had covers, pillows, and some food stashed away. She collapsed near the entrance; when she woke up Rozika was bending over her, covering her with a soft blanket, and caressing her hair.

Tension, dreadful fear, and starvation followed. There was hardly any food left in the house or to be found in the neighborhood. Despite the fact that it was very dangerous, brave Rozika snuck out of the cellar and went in search of bread, but her effort was always futile and she came back empty handed. They kept themselves hidden in the darkest corners of the basement, not knowing if they would face death yet again the next morning. The following day the cadaver of a horse that had died on the road was found near the house. People armed themselves with sharp knives and descended on the decaying animal like vultures, cutting pieces of its meat, taking away even the organs and the hide. Marita was all skin and bones and could hardly stand on her feet. She was almost too weak to lift her head and Rozika tried to feed her the boiled liver of the horse, which had been the only piece she had been able to salvage from the dead animal. Marita refused vehemently, threw up, and fainted when her aunt forced her to swallow some of it since she was worried that the young girl would die of hunger. Nobody pressured her to eat the meat from the dead horse after that because it was obvious that she was ready to die rather than put it in her mouth. And then—there was nothing left for them to eat, nothing at all, and they thought that they were doomed to die. Yet, on January 1 4, two long days after the horrible event, the Russians entered the city and salvation had come to the Jews.

Marita was very fortunate; most of her family had survived the ordeal, except for a young sister of her stepfather who was shot and whose body was thrown into the Danube. During the last days of the war, when they could no longer be sent to the concentration camps, many of the Jews were killed and their bodies disposed of by throwing them into the river. Her grandfather, who had faced the same life-threatening investigation in the yard, had also been saved by a miracle. He had passed the inspection and been permitted to join the queue of those who were not under suspicion. It was at that moment the bombs had fallen. He was shocked and shaken but nothing had happened to him and, seeing all the wounded around him, tried to aid an old man who was bleeding profusely and screaming for help. The dying man was leaning on him as he was trying to get him out of the yard. One of the officers ordered him to stop and, after looking at him closely, told him to drop the injured person and get back in the line again. However the commotion and the chaos at that time were so overwhelming that there was no longer any line and thus the officer commanded a young soldier to lead the grandfather into the house and check his private parts closely to find out whether he was circumcised. The officer was deaf to the grandfather's objections that he had already been cleared and that the injured man would die if left lying on the ground. The young soldier pushed him with the rifle and he had no choice but to enter the house. He looked at the soldier and saw a child barely grown up, in a uniform that was far too big for him—wrinkled, spotted with blood and mud—and with fear written all over his face. In the bathroom, before removing his pants as ordered by the young soldier, the grandfather took out of one of his pockets two golden coins he had received earlier as a birthday gift from his daughter—Marita's mother—and, looking into the young soldier's eyes, told him, "My son, the war is almost over. Don't dirty your hands with another crime you will have to pay for. Take these two very special coins as a reminder that you are a good person and say nothing to the officer!" The young soldier hesitated only for a moment, and then he took the coins without uttering a word and left the room. Marita's grandfather never saw him again. After the war many of the Nazis were taken to court and her grandfather testified against the officer who had headed the investigation on that fateful day. He felt that that was the right thing to be done, to punish the murderers for the unspeakable crimes they had committed.

Many years have passed but Marita cannot forget those events; she does not dwell on them continually but they are always there in the back of her mind and in the depths of her heart. Fate was kind to her and made it possible for her to survive those calamities; she is aware that one can sometimes hope for a miracle and escape what seems to be an inexorable and unyielding doom. She passed through the Holocaust like a person staggering in a snowstorm, moving slowly in between the snowflakes, without being touched by them.

Source Note

Based on the interview with Marita Feldmann in Santiago, Chile, March 2002. After the Holocaust Marita found her new home in Chile where she has been blessed with a family and a happy life. Her son Roberto is a rabbi in one of the synagogues in Santiago.

The Hatter of Cuenca

A local woman, a *chola*, walks slowly, at the same time weaving the *toquilla* leaves carefully in an intricate pattern to what will become one of her lovely Panama hats. The narrow alleys of Chordeleg, the native Indian name of Chorro de Oro, a village about fifty kilometers away from Cuenca, are dusty and somewhat twisted. Those little streets would be bleak if it were not for the colorfully dressed Indian women. They frequent them with their fiery ponchos, multicolored, beautifully embroidered blouses, and striking skirts, working at the same time, weaving and toiling at the hats, which are their main source of income. They walk, chat, and laugh, their hands move continuously, mechanically and rhythmically, but their eyes glance around and they seem to be interested mainly in the few taxis that arrive here and there bringing tourists to the area. Many of the hats rest on their heads in piles of three, four, five, and even more. They seem to sit steadily each on top of the other and very seldom form a crooked pyramid that might collapse at any time. It is quite amazing how graceful these cholas are, walking and watching the local scene with their fingers weaving continuously, without making a mistake. Most of the hats they weave are left unfinished. These are then sent to a factory in Cuenca where the straw undergoes a certain process by which the hats are finished and blocked, and finally packed according to their designs and quality, to be shipped to different places in the world.

The tall, lean gentleman who owns the most prominent hat factory in Cuenca is of German descent. His Spanish, although perfect, is not as melodious as that of the natives; it still carries the harshness of his mother tongue. He has spent most of his life in Cuenca, although he lived for some time in Colombia and still remembers Germany, his town of birth, Munich, and the way things were before the Second World War. The family had been fortunate to have come to South America before the war and escape the extermination of the Jews there, thanks to an uncle who had settled down in Bogota. The uncle, while in Germany, had been sick with the influenza that killed thousands in 1919, which made it imperative for him to seek warmer climes. Thus he spent the European winters in the balmy climate of Colombia taking care of his health, and traveled back to Germany only during the summers. Initially, the uncle had sold watches, toys, and other items manufactured in Germany, but later on switched to the hat business that promised to be very profitable, as indeed it did. The nephew followed in his uncle's footsteps and eventually moved and made his residence in Cuenca, which was and continues to be the capital of the Panama hat manufacturing industry.

The hatter has become a much-revered citizen of the small town, influential and very comfortable. He was honored as the president of the Chamber of Commerce in Cuenca and is fortunate to count very powerful individuals among his friends. He was invited to represent the tiny Jewish community as part of the welcoming group that greeted the Pope when he visited Cuenca. The archbishop is one of his best friends, with whom he enjoys exchanging jokes. His eyes twinkle when he talks about it and emphasizes that those jokes are not necessarily religious ones, and that priests have at times a sense of humor, which allows him to tell them tales that are not always "kosher." He cannot resist but describe one of the incidents when the archbishop asked him to tell a particular joke to an important visiting cardinal. There were hundreds of people waiting for the cardinal's blessing and the hatter felt uncomfortable and somewhat embarrassed to tell a joke under those circumstances. However, the archbishop insisted and so he complied. The cardinal listened, smiled, and kept a straight face; after all, nobody knew what the hatter was whispering to him; that was the secret! And what was the joke? A rabbi and a bishop were having dinner together. The bishop offered the rabbi a pork dish, at which time the rabbi explained that pork was not allowed to be eaten according to Jewish law. The bishop commented that it was such a pity since the meat was a most delicious thing. When they parted the rabbi asked the bishop to give regards to his wife. The surprised bishop remarked that his religion would not permit him to get married! The rabbi commented that it was such a pity, since it was a most delicious thing . . .

Although being traditional and following the rules of the Jewish religion with an open heart, the hatter is not overzealous and knows when to bend the rules. He laughs when he explains that he does not need a yarmulke while attending services since he wears every day, without fail, his hairpiece. As a matter of fact, he adds, he has quite a collection and can choose a different style on any given day.

The hatter's wife is a lovely lady who, unfortunately, suffers from Parkinson's disease but is, nevertheless, a fighter who does not give in. She used to be very active socially and still is able to converse and entertain, and runs her household and the people who work for her very efficiently. The office of the hatter is full of happy family photographs, children's and grandchildren's as well as the folks from the old country. There are also displays of many framed certificates of excellence that attest to his importance and value, not only to the Jewish community in Cuenca but also to the one in Quito. Over there, in the capital of Ecuador, not only he but also his sons are very influential and respected members of a much bigger and prosperous Jewish community.

The Jewish community—if one may call it that—in Cuenca consists now of just two families, the hatter's and another one which is actually only half Jewish since the wife is a gentile, yet whose children have been brought up according to Jewish customs. During the Second World War there lived a few Jewish families in Cuenca—Holocaust victims who had been lucky enough to escape from Europe with their lives intact and sometimes just a little of their fortunes. Some of those people were Czechs and Germans, and some—just a handful—were Polish. Initially, they rented a building that served them as a synagogue. They became close, since there were so few of them, and tried to contribute to good causes such as Israel and to support the needy ones among themselves, as well as in other places in Ecuador. They felt forgotten and somewhat lost in the middle of Ecuador, high up in the Andes, but were grateful to be still alive.

The hatter's main achievement is the restoration of the Jewish cemetery in town. During and after the Second World War, the Jews were buried outside the existing Christian cemetery and there was no wall around the graves. It was a dreadful place and all foreigners were cast in that lot, which was used as a dump as well. Nobody wanted to visit there and the neglect lasted for some years until the hatter could not take it anymore. He approached the municipality of the city of Cuenca asking for permission to build a wall around the Jewish graves. It was granted mainly because of the fact that the Vice-Alcade of Cuenca was a contractor who was interested in the project. A tall, yellow fence was erected, creating a small enclave within the large Christian graveyard, protecting the tiny cemetery from vandalism. Now there are mature trees on the plot, most of the graves are tended, and the paths clear of weeds, making it possible for visitors to walk around. There are two entrances to the Jewish cemetery, one from the street, which is on a somewhat higher elevation with a few steps to descend, and across from this entrance is another gate separating it from the Christian graveyard. Both gates are locked and, accessible only with the permission of the hatter, the cemetery has been the property of the Jewish community in Cuenca for the last twenty years. The oldest graves date to the first decades of the twentieth century. The site has become a world unto itself; the tales of most of those resting there forgotten forever. One still remembered is that of a family of three—a mother, father, and their son. Tragedy had struck and the father and son were killed in an accident. The despondent mother could not accept the cruel ordeal and took her own life. She was buried far from the father and the son since Jewish law forbids those who commit suicide from being buried within the boundaries of the Jewish graveyard; instead they must be buried outside it. When the plot was purchased and the fence erected, it so happened that it also included the spot where the unfortunate mother was buried. Thus, whether it was the Almighty's doing or maybe just mere chance, her resting place has ended up within the walls of the Jewish graveyard where she found, finally, lasting peace.

The Cuencanos are supposedly not superstitious but they have a great respect for the forces of nature and are very intense in their religious beliefs and practices. While visiting the Jewish cemetery, I noticed a very old man standing by the fence and looking in. His dark face was lined and wrinkled due to years of labor and exposure to the sun but his dark eyes were wide open and his curiosity quite obvious even from afar. He tilted his hat backwards, as if he did not want to miss a thing, and remained glued to the fence for as long as he saw people walking around the graves. When I got out of the gate, he was still standing there and smiled at me, showing only a couple of yellow teeth that were all that remained in his mouth. I approached him and he crossed himself. I do not think he thought of me as an evil force, but seeing me coming out of the non-Christian cemetery and a foreigner at that, he must have decided to take precautions, just in case.

When I addressed him in Spanish he seemed pleasantly surprised. I told him I was a writer and that it would be really wonderful if he could tell me something about Cuenca, any kind of stories he could remember. He sat down on the pavement, his back leaning on the yellow cemetery fence, and asked if I knew the meaning of the name Cuenca, which is the most important town of the district of Azuay. Without waiting for my answer, he told me that the town initially had the ancient indigenous name of Wapdondelik, which meant "wide plain like the sky." Other names followed and all of them described the territory as a broad area; some sounded more poetic than others, but finally, in the sixteenth century, the town was given the Spanish name of Cuenca from the Latin word for shell—an area surrounded by mountains. The official name of the city is also "Santa Ana of the Four Rivers of Cuenca," since it sits amidst four rivers. I was thrilled that I had, just by chance, found a person who knew so much about the town and asked him to tell me some more. It was a mild, pleasant afternoon and he did not seem to be in any rush.

Japo did not tell me much about Jews that had lived in Cuenca—he only remembered one that had been a peddler and walked around with a parrot on his shoulder, a friendly, popular man—but Japo was a treasure as far as other stories were concerned. He told me about a large, heavyset man who many years ago had been the barber as well as the dentist in town. In those long forgotten days, people who suffered from toothache had to ask the barber to remove them. The dentist/barber used to give them a very strong dose of Chicha, their favorite fermented drink, and then slap them a few times so that the patient became groggy and almost unconscious. After that he removed the decayed tooth with pliers and gave the poor patient another dose of the drink, which made him sleep off the pain (disinfect the wound as well) and wake up next morning once again in love with life. This dentist/barber, said Japo, was most probably Jewish, since his name was Elias. He had suffered from a kidney disease that made him incontinent. For that reason, he carried around his waist, concealed within his pants, a can that prevented him from being embarrassed in public. When he was dying in the local hospital, he asked for his pillow since he, supposedly, could not sleep without it. After his death they discovered many bills inside, money that had been collected over the years and had lost all its value to inflation. The man died childless and so did the story of his life; nobody but a few elderly people remember the tale. Yes, Japo said once again, he was most probably a Jew.

Japo became quite uneasy when a few insects landed on his bare arm. He swept them away and seemed to be quite agitated until he got rid of them. We moved to another section of the fence that was more shaded, where only a few rays of the sun filtered through the branches of a tall, dense tree. Free of the annoying mosquitoes, he apologized and told me he had always been afraid of insects, any flying kind, since he had heard as a child his mother telling the story of the Nigua. It seems many years ago, a certain mean, little insect called Nigua tortured the people of Cuenca. It was very tiny, resembled a flea, but had a much longer sting, a gigantic "trompa" snout, Japo explained. It penetrated under the skin of animals and people, where it deposited its eggs that caused severe itching and ulcers. It had to be removed right away before it caused serious damage or even death. The story goes that one particular woman, who lived in those distant days, was very unfortunate to have a nigua embedded in one of her breasts. Being very modest, she did not want to tell anybody about it; rather she grinned and bore it for a few weeks until she died of it. Women in those days had quite secluded lives and kept to themselves. Only midwives were highly respected since there were very few of them, and it was unheard of for a woman to deliver her baby with the help of a male doctor.

"More stories about women?" I asked. Yes, said Japo. There was the tale of two sisters who had opened a bakery and whose bread had been extremely popular in Cuenca. They baked the bread for many years and people lined the street in front of the shop early every morning to get the bread before they ran out of it. One day the shoppers found the bakery closed. Their concern was genuine; they worried about the welfare of the sisters and also could not imagine living without their favorite baked goods. Nevertheless, they had to get used to it since the two sisters had come down with leprosy and left the town soon afterwards. The people of Cuenca lived in fear for a long time until they calmed down and accepted the fact that the disease was not contagious. Japo himself was not sure that it is really true, but there have been no cases of leprosy in Cuenca for many years, so nobody worries about it anymore.

I spent the afternoon with Japo and, when asked where I could find him in case I wanted to talk to him again, he said I should come to the same place at the cemetery as he lived nearby. I watched him as he disappeared around the corner of a street and then realized that I had been so involved in his storytelling that I had failed to ask him about himself or his family. It occurred to me that, since he also had not asked me about myself, it was perhaps appropriate not to pry into a person's private life in that far corner of the world. I looked for Japo again during the last days of my visit. I went to the graveyard several times, at different hours, and waited for him to appear, but he did not. I asked around, wondering if somebody saw him, but all I got was a blank stare and a negative answer; nobody knew a man by the name of Japo who fitted his description. I never saw him again.

The hat factory is a low, spread out building with a big sign at the entrance. It is located in a rather drab, industrial part of town where one can find many other manufacturing workshops that blend into each other. The hatter has been in the business for many years and knows all about the Panama hat history.[1] According to legend, the hat was woven and worn first by the Incas when they discovered the amazing flexibility of the toquilla plant. The fronds of the palm are separated into the strands that weavers use in the final product by means of a laborious process that involves peeling, boiling, and drying. The plant is found in other South and Central American countries but it seems that the best conditions for its growth are in the coastal lowlands of Ecuador. The hat became known as the Panama hat only in the last century when laborers who were working on the Panama Canal used the Ecuadoran manufactured head cover to protect themselves from the burning sun. It became most fashionable after members of the English royalty took a fancy to it and when president Theodore Roosevelt was photographed wearing such a hat while touring the Panama Canal construction site in 1906.

The workers in the hatter's factory are local people, some of them the descendants of weavers who were considered artists in their own right. Today the art of weaving is disappearing, as well as the ancient knowledge of blocking and shaping that makes the true "Panama" hat so flexible and smooth with an exceptionally uniform color and tightness of weave. The purists among the workers refuse to use the modern machines for blocking and would rather work harder and longer doing the task by hand. It might also be that, in a way, they are afraid of the monstrous, metal creatures that want to take over their work and maybe, in time, even steal their jobs. Displayed in the hatter's office are a few of the old, black, very heavy coal irons that were exclusively used in the past to block the hats. The factory produces the very best but also some lesser quality hats that are more affordable. One of the ways to detect a cheaper hat is to count the rings or "vueltas" on the hat. The more vueltas, the finer the hat, as it indicates how many strands have been used in the weaving process. The shapes of the hats also differ and it takes an expert to know the many intricacies involved in the creation of the finest Panama hats. Although most of the weavers no longer insist on working—as they used to in the old days due to superstitions—only under the light of the moon or when the weather is overcast, dipping their fingers constantly in cold water, it still takes a long time to produce a perfect hat: the difference between a mediocre and very fine one being the amount of time put into its creation.

The evening before I left Cuenca, I walked along the river Tomebamba, which is one of the four rivers that cross and encircle the town. The ancient Inca name of Tumipampa ("River Valley of Knives") had been the name of their ancient capital, not just the name of the river itself. The Tomebamba cuts the city in two, to the north the old town of Cuenca with its colonial homes, to the south the new section. The other river, Machangara, is the city's northern border; the Yanuncay and the Tarqui flow through the southern suburbs. It was cool and the water was calm, the waves flowing smoothly and peacefully following their natural course. Here and there one could see a few women still laundering their clothes and gathering them in big baskets. It was hard to believe, at that moment, that the hatter had called the Tomebamba a demented river, one which had to do with its history of flooding that devastated the town many times in its past. Nevertheless, I could picture the hatter on one of those disastrous days, helping a friend of his to safety by pulling him off the raging river. He had mentioned the incident only in passing and, in his modesty, would not admit that he had done a heroic act and saved a human being from death. He had just smiled, shrugged his shoulders and, with a wave of goodbye, went off to check the lock at the gate of his factory that was closing at nightfall.

Source Note

Based partially on an interview with Mr. Kurt Dorfzaun, Cuenca, Ecuador, in August 2001.

Text Note

1. Some sources on the history of the Panama hat: "History of hats—The Hat Site," *http://www.thehatsite.com/panama.html*; "The Montecristi Fino—The Finest Straw Hat in the World," *http://www.finofino.com/Panamas.html*; "On Top—A Montecristi is the Best Panama Hat but for how much longer?" by Harry Rosenholtz, *http://www.cigaraficionado.com*.

Icarus the Frog

*I*n the old days when animals were still able to talk, Rana Icarus, the frog, looked different from the way she appears today. She was round and fat and, although small and not very prominent among the other creatures, was pleased with herself and proud of her intense green coloring. One day there circulated an invitation among the animals of the world— a bountiful party was to be held in the heavens, yet exclusively only for those who could fly. Rana felt insulted and left out but, being stubborn and cunning, made up her mind to attend the festivities no matter what.

The crow lived nearby and Rana decided to visit him to ask for his advice. When she approached his dwelling, she found him cleaning and tuning his guitar and called out his name. He barely turned his head and did not respond to her polite: *"Bom dia Senhor,"* meaning *"Good day, Sir."* Looking sulky and gruff, he told her to leave since he was busy: *"Vai, nao tenho tempo."* Rana felt humiliated but it made her desire to go to the party even stronger. Watching Mr. Crow handling his precious guitar and cackling away, getting ready for his performance, she suddenly had an idea. She waited patiently for him to finish his practice. When he dozed off, she quickly jumped into the guitar case and hid in a corner. Mr. Crow woke up, closed the case, fluffed up his feathers, and polished his beak just before taking off for the party. While airborne he had a feeling that his guitar weighed more than usual but did not give it too much thought. He just came to the conclusion that he was getting old, unable to carry as much as he used to, and that made him pretty sad.

Rana had a wonderful time at the party. She hopped out of the case without anyone noticing since there was such a large crowd present and so many sounds to be heard. She spent the whole time eating and drinking to her heart's content until she fell asleep in a cozy little cloud. When Rana woke up, all the flying animals had left; it was dark except for a few twinkling stars and there was heavenly silence everywhere. She started weeping in despair since she knew that without wings there was no way she could return to her pond. An angel was passing by and heard the desolate sound of the croaking Rana. He took pity on her and furnished her with a pair of wings made out of wax. He attached them to her body and warned her to fly back to earth before the sun came out. Rana expressed her deep gratitude and, feeling relieved that her troubles were over, dozed off once again. When she woke up the second time, the sun was already up and it was getting warm. Rana quickly spread her wings and started the descent to earth. The sunrays were getting hotter by the minute, the wax started melting and dripping off the wings, and Rana began falling down very quickly. Being of a kind nature, she screamed to warn creatures on the ground to get out of the way and not be hurt. Of course, she was also terrified and desperately cried out, "*Socorro. Socorro,*" not knowing from where help could come this time. She saw a big, dark object right underneath her and fell with a big bang on what turned out to be a huge stone. Rana recovered from her injuries but was never the same again. Her soft, round body was flattened a great deal and she never regained her old looks. Nevertheless, to this day she feels grateful for being alive and feels more comfortable croaking at night, when the sun does not shine.[1]

Source Note

Based on IFA (Israeli Folktale Archives) # 11226, a Brazilian tale told by Nurit Bakar (from Kibbutz Haain) and recorded by Ronit Beigl. It is an unusual variant of the Greek myth of Icarus.

Text Note

1. African oral tradition has a somewhat similar tale, "Tortoise and the Birds," where the tortoise manages to infiltrate a feast that the birds are having in the sky and consumes all the food. The tortoise is punished; it falls from the sky, and its shell broken into pieces. At the end, a medicine man finds the suffering creature and patches up its shell. It is possible that this Brazilian tale's origin is also in Africa since that continent's oral tradition has many ancient narratives (such as the Anansi spider tales) that try to make sense of the world and explain different phenomena (*http://www.cocc.edu/cagatuccci/classes/hum211/afstory.htm*).

Patches from the Past

$\mathcal{T}$he small town of Biecz in Poland was founded a long time ago by the beloved Queen Jadwiga.[1] Legend tells us that once, while the queen was riding a horse and visiting rural areas of her country, she dropped the whip at a certain place and paused for a moment. She then turned to her entourage and told them that she had decided to found a village at that very site. It is in this small place, near the border of the former Czechoslovakia, where Shabtai was born in 1934.

The family was very large; Shabtai's father had eleven siblings and his mother four. His paternal grandfather owned a *dvur*—a farm—and every summer the family got together. It felt as if a whole battalion had descended on the manor; there were as many as fifty relatives and the small village of about three thousand people was always aware of the big gatherings at their family homestead. The dvur stood at the end of an unsurfaced road, the dust rose high up into the sky for miles, and took a long time to dissipate after the guests, in their vehicles, reached their destination. His grandfather was quite wealthy but very frugal and cautious with his money. One of his sons, Shabtai's uncle, managed the farm for him. It was like a small enclave within the village where many peasants worked for the old man. When he was in a good mood and the family was visiting, he summoned all the children to the dining room and promised them a treat. From a hidden place he brought out a small iron chest, which was secured with a big, rusty, dangling lock, and opened it slowly, watching the children who stood there in awe. He took out small lumps of brown sugar and gave one to each child, who readily kissed his hand. Sugar was not, necessarily, their favorite sweet but the kiss was the price the thrifty grandfather seemed to demand for his gift.

On Saturdays the town went dead since half of the population was Jewish. They were not orthodox in their way of lives, nor were they reformed Jews but felt a need to adjust to the modern times. Although they did not keep all of the rules at home, such as eating kosher foods, not smoking cigars, etc., they felt an emotional urge and obligation to observe the basic traditions in public. Life in the *shtetl* was very vibrant before World War II; there were many political movements and young people held meetings in many places, including the local library.

When the war broke out, most of the grown men in the family fled east to Russia with the retreating Soviet troops. The women and children stayed in their hometown. It was a great hardship since Shabtai's father was gone, leaving his family behind. Food supplies were scarce and they had to survive on very little. Many of their possessions were sold in order to buy food. In 1940, when the Germans invaded Russia, the order was given for all Jews to return to their place of origin.

Shabtai has always had a "memoria corrida"—a "running memory"— of many events since he was two or three years old, but he has more "flares" than anything else; he sees certain pictures flashing through his mind and one of these "photos" he sees more often than others. He remembers vividly his father coming back, one cold day in November. It had been snowing lightly and he was looking out of the window at the gray, bleak landscape that surrounded the farm when, suddenly, he saw a small, dark figure advancing slowly along the frozen road.

The figure grew and became bigger and bigger until the boy realized that the man was not a stranger but his own father whom he had not seen for many months. That evening their dwelling was filled with joy and gratitude, and he will never forget the Hanukkah he spent that year with his father. Their happiness did not last long since, shortly after the holiday, another order was given by the Germans forcing all the Jewish men to return to the same places in Russia where they had been before. His father had no choice but to obey and left with a heavy heart, not knowing whether he would ever see his family again. He never did; that was the last time they saw him. They tried to find him and locate his whereabouts after the war, mainly in a place called Kolomeia—close to the Russian border—which had had a big Jewish ghetto, but failed time after time. They never found him and he was lost to them forever.

When the Russians liberated the area, the Jews in town had a grim task to perform, which was to clear the streets of all the cadavers and give the Jews among them proper burials. While helping with that solemn task, Shabtai thought of his father who was lost and who—God knows where—must have found his death in a foreign land and was buried, most probably, in a mass grave without the proper rites. It is that thought which causes him great pain, and weighs on him particularly during the High Holidays, especially at Yom Kippur. In those days the town functioned as one entity, everybody helped everybody without fail. He nods his head slowly, his deep brown eyes darken even more, and he says sadly, "Such solidarity does not exist anymore."

After the war his mother had to cope with very difficult times. His grandparents were still alive but in bad health, and Shabtai's mother tried to run a hardware store they owned without much success. She had a relative in Bolivia who agreed to help them, but they first had to move to France, since Poland did not have a Bolivian consulate and the papers were sent to Paris. The year was 1947 and they arrived in Bolivia after having endured a harsh, long voyage on a ship named *Campana*, which took them to the port of Rio de Janeiro. It was a very old ship that had been fixed up so that it could carry over four hundred people. They slept in bunks that were piled up in three levels and the food was atrocious. He remembers being ravenous at first but then, after a while, his stomach could not digest the foul food anymore and, mercifully, he stopped feeling hungry. Shabtai closes his eyes and describes another flash he sees on his memory's screen; this time they are in an airplane flown by the airline Panagra taking them to the capital of Bolivia, La Paz. Panagra, Pan American-Grace Airways, Inc., was the first airline to fly big propeller planes across South America, starting in 1928, and Shabtai never forgot the extraordinary experience of his first flight.

In Bolivia his mother started a hardware store, since she had had some experience in that field, and was able to succeed thanks mainly to the help of her relative. It was in La Paz that she met her second husband who had a son from a previous marriage. Shabtai did not have any special feelings toward his stepfather who was a decent man; yet, somehow, it did not matter to him, one way or another, whether he was a kind man or not. Shabtai is a very reserved man and words do not come to him easily. He tries to explain this indifference as being a result of the war—people trained and forced themselves to be numb; they cultivated this kind of immunity against sensitivity so as not to succumb to grief and sorrow. It was like an illness that lingered with all of those who had survived, and it was a chronic malady, in a sense, from which they could never recover. It is hard to get used to feelings of joy and expect happiness when there is a continual fear that they are just illusions which will vanish in no time, leaving us even more miserable than before.

Shabtai was quite content in Bolivia. Until then his life had been a series of fragments from the very beginning and he felt that maybe he had finally discovered a path that would lead him to a better place in the future. He still did not settle down and left for Israel, where he stayed until he was twenty-four years old. There he worked in a print shop—Ha Madpis Hamemshalti—for two-and-a-half years but decided to return to Bolivia to help his mother in her shop. In 1958 he moved to Peru, where at first he opened a shoe store that was not too successful and left him on the verge of starvation. He then became a traveling sales-man—a peddler—like many other European Jews, and traveled in the provinces of Peru selling different kinds of merchandise. Shabtai's face lights up with a rare smile and he calls himself an "Ali Baba" with just a few suitcases full of merchandise but with no great or exotic adventures to boast about. Nevertheless, he was successful selling clothes, fabrics, and jewelry—anything and everything people were interested in. Two years later, he was able to open another shop. From then on things improved; his new shop, which handled electrical goods, brought him good fortune and, when he married and had two children, a son and a daughter, his happiness was complete. Finally, he felt he was not sitting on suitcases anymore and that he could store them away. His wife is a convert, which is not unusual in Jewish circles in Peru, and feels very comfortable within the community. He has been happily married for thirty-three years and has no romantic story to tell about their first encounter. All beginnings, he proclaims, are romantic and promising. "What is happiness?" he wonders. "Is it like a river that flows, or rather sparks, flickers of light that vanish almost as soon as they appear?"

Converts into Judaism are quite common in Peru; at times the reactions of some Jews are not of solidarity but, in general, there is no problem. It takes about a generation to "melt" in. There are some native Peruvians who feel that they are the descendants of the Marranos who fled from Spain during the Inquisition. Many of them have converted into Judaism and left for Israel. A friend of Shabtai, from the city of Cajamarka, who carries the name Rocasela, shows some inclination towards Judaism. His father had been told by his father never to change his name, promising him that one day he would understand why. It might still be a mystery to him, says Shabtai, but actually is quite simple to understand. It comes from the Hebrew word *sela*, which means rock, and so there should be no doubt that he is of Jewish stock. Shabtai feels that one religion is not necessarily better than another, but a family with children always has to supply guidance and direction. The concept of what a family is has changed. A bit of the "old" Judaism is slowly disintegrating. It is like a certain flower, he says, that does not like to be handled. It closes its petals if you touch it; but if you leave it alone, just water it properly, and put it in the sun, it might not grow as much as it used to, but it will, nevertheless, stay green and survive. In Israel, he comments, religion seems to be more a source of power rather than ideology but it is also true, for some reason, that one does not feel the need to worship there the way one does in the diaspora. In Lima, Jews feel the need to go to the temple more often and he does so too. If an orthodox person tries to pressure him to follow certain rituals, which he thinks are either inappropriate or exaggerated, he simply tells him in Hebrew, "Ata lo tagia la shamayim darki," meaning "you won't reach heaven through me . . ."

The temple where we met, one of the four Jewish synagogues in Lima, is actually a building within a building. The inner sanctuary, almost the whole synagogue, was built within the shell—the walls of an outer, previously existing edifice of Grecian style. It has been completely renovated and painted with a bright, yellow color that shines and shimmers when the sun hits it. The iron gate has a lock with a small window on the adjacent wall; the guard can thus examine visitors' identification papers before admitting them. Flowers in pots adorn the entrance; they are well taken care of, and the deep, green color of their broad leaves enhances the golden glow of the house.

I can still see the one and only old photograph Shabtai showed me— the image of a beautiful, young woman with large, dark, sorrowful eyes, displaying an unusual, quilted dress. The photo, black and white, and faded as well, did not do justice to the garment that, nevertheless, showed the craftsmanship of the woman, Shabtai's mother, who had made it herself. She had worked on it almost every day during the war; since it was the only dress that she had left, it had to be "darned" like a torn pair of socks in order to keep it from falling apart. Each piece of material in the quilted dress tells a story of its own; each stitch describes the grief she felt while working on it; the threads illustrate the hardships of daily life and the fear of the coming days. Frayed around the edges, this is not a fancy quilt that gentile women enjoyed working on and considered a pleasant feminine pastime. It does not have the style, the scheme, or the color pattern of a lovely crafted piece but it is, rather, a collection of scraps of history, patches from the past, that tell a very original and touching tale of its own and, as such, it is priceless.

Source Note

Based on an interview with Shabtai Stein in Lima, Peru, August 2001. Shabtai's mother's dress is on display at the Museum of Jewish Heritage in New York.

Text Note

1. Queen Jadwiga (1373–1399) was the daughter of the Hungarian King Louis who inherited the throne of Poland when his cousin, the great king Casimire, passed away. After Louis' death, the young Jadwiga, at the time only eleven years old, was crowned as the ruler of Poland. Her reputation as a wise and fair monarch, adored by her people, is legendary.

The Diver

The young rabbi's intense blue eyes lit up when he talked about the summer camp where the everlasting connection to his European past became intertwined with the love and devotion to the country he was born in and to the culture and history of Chile. It took place some years ago in the south, near Concepcion,[1] in the Bio-Bio river area, famous for its white water rafting and the beauty of the Andean countryside surrounding it.[2] The camp, organized by a young Argentinean rabbi named Angel Kleinman, was set close to the place where the mighty river, carving its way through spectacular canyons, merges into the Pacific Ocean. Staying in a small dilapidated and crumbling building that served as a school, the youth found spiritual nourishment and a sense of stability he had never experienced outside its unstable walls. Many peasant huts surrounded the adobe structure and he was able to feast his eyes on the splendid wildflowers, various kinds of beautiful trees, and the slow flying crimson-backed buzzards found in that area. He was enchanted listening to the Bio-Bio bird, whose subtle song— "bioooo-bioooo"—has given the name to the river. Most of all he felt an affinity to the streams of the river and the tides of the ocean as if they had a special meaning to him, as indeed they did.

The rabbi recalls a ballad that the famous German poet Friedrich Schiller had written many years ago, "Der Taucher"—"The Diver," which is one of the European links he has inherited and which has touched his heart.[3] In this epic poem, a cruel king challenges a young man to jump into the depths of the foaming, raging ocean and retrieve a golden goblet he had thrown into it. The chalice would then become the youth's property. It was a most precious object, one of a kind, if lost never to be found again. The brave man dives into the menacing waters of the savage sea and miraculously is able to find the golden cup and bring it back to the surface, where he presents it to the king. The harsh monarch, nevertheless, is not satisfied and casting the goblet a second time into the seething waters, challenges the youth once again to find it, this time also promising him his daughter's hand as a reward. The youth warns the king of the fatal perils of the depths, yet complies, but this time he does not return.

The rabbi has been deeply inspired by the ballad—its profound meaning and insight into the dangers lurking in the human mind—yet to him the poem is precious for a different reason. To him the goblet symbolizes the faith people carry in their hearts but lose at times. He has dived into the depths of his own past and found the goblet of his forefather's beliefs. Polishing it and safeguarding it from any damage, he has not only reaffirmed the old traditions but also inserted new elements, new shapes, new colors, and new ideas without harming the old ones. He has created a vibrant, fresh congregation, a Jewish enclave in the New World based on and saturated with the ancient revered rules. Unlike Schiller's protagonist he does not intend to give away the precious goblet he has found or lose it, but will always guard it with his life and soul. By reclaiming the old and intertwining it with the new, the rabbi has come to his own fulfillment as a human being and as a teacher to his people.

The river affected him deeply and so did the campsite that was full of an unbelievable energy he had never experienced before. The camp, named *Maboy Eliyahu*, was situated near a hill that overlooks the ocean that, at various times in history, had been the homestead of the Spanish conquerors as well as native Chileans.[4] It is also the place where the famous surgeon Francisco Maldonaldo de Silva had prayed day after day to the God of his forefathers. Francisco, a crypto-Jew, the son of a famous doctor with the same name, had fled from Lima, Peru (around 1630) to the south of Chile to hide from the shadows of the Inquisition. He had settled down in this Marrano outpost in the relatively remote part of the Spanish Empire where for a while he found peace. Legend tells us that every day he used to find solace all alone at the base of the same hill where the Jewish summer camp was located centuries later. He asked God for strength and courage to enable him to keep his Jewish faith and escape harm. The rabbi did not know this at the time of his stay at the camp and understood only later the immense magnetism emanating from that place. Francisco Maldonaldo de Silva has earned not only an esteemed reputation in history but also left a deep, indelible mark on that particular spot.[5]

The rabbi has followed the calling he took upon himself and helps not just his own congregation but also those who are in particular need of his guidance. In the middle of the Mapuche's land, around the towns of Curacautin, Cunco, and Gorbea, bordering on the old region of Araucania, he found a group of people who have considered themselves members of the *Inglesia Israelita*—the *Israel Church*—since the late 1800s. It is an odd name to be adopted by a small group of people who cannot prove who they are but who do follow certain rules and habits of Judaism with great zest. The rabbi came to the conclusion that there existed not a genealogical chain of transmission but a chain of transmission nevertheless. These were probably descendants of the Marranos, who had lived there many years ago, and clung to certain Judaic customs for generations. It was not rabbinical material that had been transmitted but rather just the most basic Biblical knowledge. They could not prove much since crypto-Jews were always careful to erase anything that hinted at their hidden beliefs; the only obvious clue that has remained is the name Israelita strangely attached to the word Iglesia, going back to the times when the Catholic church did not even exist in that part of the continent. The rabbi met with the successors of these Marranos, and gathered many tales that pointed in the direction of Judaic worship despite the lack of genealogical connection. On Friday evenings, a Mapuche mother would return to her *ruca*—a hut made of straw and wood—with a wicker basket full of pine nuts, which is a staple of their diet, and light candles at sunset without knowing the reason. She would also pray and insert into her melodic Mapuche chant words such as *"Ribono Shel Olam"* or *"Hashem"* and Biblical names like Abraham and David.

Many of these families, living in very remote areas, had not converted to Judaism despite their apparent, but perhaps vague, connection. They were already being discriminated against by other groups of natives and adding on the yoke of Judaism—the conversion following the formal

Halacha—would have increased their vulnerability. In a way, encouraging them to convert would have been playing on their naiveté, confusing them and, in the end, causing them to be completely rejected by their tribes. However, there were other families within the *Inglesia Israelita* that did convert to Judaism with the help of the rabbi and some of his colleagues. These individuals, from the area around the town of Temuco, were drawn to Judaism in a very profound way. They clung to the very hazy origins of their church, which had gone through many mysterious stages. In the nineteenth century the *Inglesia* had been full of crypto-Jewish features to which, later on, many Christian beliefs were added. They had struggled with questions such as the nature of Jesus' role in the church and whether he was indeed the Messiah. The rejection of some of these concepts led to the establishment of the *Congregacion Israelita de Dios Unico—Israel Congregation of the Only God*—and *Bnei Noah—Sons of Noah*. Although there was still some connection to Jesus, some of the members rejected even those ideas and traveled to Santiago for actual conversion to Judaism.

Sadly, the Jewish community of Temuco has not accepted this group very willingly. Temuco, capital of the Cautin province on the river by the same name, was founded in 1881. This oldest Jewish community in Chile consists of people that came from Greece, Macedonia, Turkey, Salonika, and Monastir. They brought with them centuries-old ideas and habits as well as a sense of ingrained fear and an intense awareness of the need for self-defense. It was very difficult for them to accept dark-faced strangers who claimed to be of Jewish origin but had nothing to prove their lineage. Without possessing Jewish ethnic elements, the newcomers faced discrimination and, at times, hostility or even disdain. Every month the rabbi traveled to see them and taught them all that was necessary for their conversion. He tried to be realistic and knew the many obstacles in his way, but for him the main issue was the fact that these people truly believed they were of Jewish stock and had the endurance and fortitude to pursue the dream of going back to their roots. Each year they travel with their families to Santiago to join the congregation for the High Holidays. It is always an immense hardship for them since they are quite poor but they still do it willingly. They have adopted special names such as Cabanistas—the booth builders—since they have an enormous interest in building the Succah and dwell in it exclusively for the eight days during the holiday. Some of them are called the Sabatistas since their main concern is to keep the Shabbat according to Jewish tradition and pray so as to accelerate the second coming of the Messiah. All these people are aware that they are not the only pseudo-Jews left in the world, yet they follow everything Jewish in a fundamentalist way that is, nevertheless, far from being fanatic.

On Friday evenings, the rabbi leads his small congregation in prayer and in song. The villa where he conducts his service is a beautiful place that conforms to his ideas of combining the ancient and the new. It is the ideal synagogue—gathering place—for the young and the old, the house of prayer where the conservative and the reformed blend together without affecting each other's identity. The *drasha*—sermon—for the week that he has prepared is to them like a loaf of fresh bread. The feeling of peace and joy envelopes the area as the rabbi plays an old Jewish Shabbat melody on the sweet sounding *charango*, the little Andean guitar.

Source Note
Based on an interview with Rabbi Roberto Feldmann in Santiago, Chile, March 2002.

Text Notes
1. Concepción – A settlement founded by the *conquistador* Pedro Valdivia in 1550 after overcoming heavy resistance from the indigenous Indians, the Arucanians as the Spanish called them or the Mapuches of Southern Chile—the people of the earth—as they call themselves.

2. Bio-Bio's days as a free flowing river are numbered. A hydroelectric dam, the first of six planned, has been erected and a string of spectacular rapids has already been blocked. This project threatens not only the endangered species that can be still found in the forests of that area, the disappearing white water rafting, and tourism, but also, most tragically, dwellings of the remaining population of Mapuche tribes who have been the inhabitants of that part of the world for centuries and have nowhere else to go.

3. "Der Taucher" ("The Diver") – Friedrich Schiller's (1759–1805) famous epic poem. Franz Schubert (1797–1828) wrote a musical setting to this well-known ballad.

4. Maboy Eliyahu – The name of the summer camp is an acronym for Mate Bombilla Yerba: mate—the gourd (feminine symbol), bombilla—the metal straw (masculine symbol), and yerba—the herb. Eliyahu has the same numeric value as maboy—mystical meaning—to create. Mate is the name of a beverage, commonly consumed in many countries in Latin America. Basically it is an infusion based on an herb called Yerba Mate and usually taken with hot water. Mate is also the name of the container where the infusion is prepared or poured in and taken. Mates are made out of gourds or wood; the straws are mostly metallic or made out of bone. The drink originally consisted of Yerba Mate only but is nowadays a combination of many kinds of herbs.

5. Guillermo Blanco, a noted Chilean writer, described Francisco Maldonaldo de Silva's life in his well-known book, *Camisa Limpia*.

A Girl with Rosy Cheeks

Aida learned to milk cows at the age of thirteen when she joined her aunt on the farm and had to adjust to the new surroundings fairly quickly. She had been born in the town of Mogliev-Podolsk in Moldavia, near the Dniester river, toward the end of the nineteenth century, lived with her parents and siblings in a small house in town, and helped them run a modest grocery shop. When Aida's father died of cholera at the young age of thirty-two, her mother sent her to live with an aunt in the countryside since she could not take care of all her three children. Aida was a lovely girl, tall for her age, and well built. Her dark hair, shining black eyes, and fair complexion were enhanced by rosy cheeks, which became even more pronounced in the healthy environment of the farm. Few Jews worked the land in Moldavia in those days since they were not considered citizens and were not allowed to purchase it. Thus, they dwelt mostly in cities or towns, where they engaged in local commerce and, at times, in liquor distilling. Some of them, though, despite the discrimination against them, were able to move to the countryside and work as estate managers for landlords who owned large farms. That was what Aida's aunt did and was very successful at it. She was a very assertive, hard-working woman who had gained the respect of the landlord as well as her co-workers, most of whom were not Jewish. Unlike the Jews who lived in town, the aunt and her niece did not, initially, suffer from prejudice based on anti-Semitic myths and made friends who helped them overcome many problems as time went by.

Aida worked quite hard taking care of the animals on the farm, tending the vegetable garden, and helping her aunt with some cooking. The landlord raised cattle as well as sheep, and grew wheat, barley, corn, sugar beets, grapes, and sunflowers. The nobleman also had a daughter whom he was very concerned about since the young girl was of a sickly disposition, very pale and weak. When Aida arrived at the farm and he noticed her energy and cheerfulness, he asked her to come every day to the house and play with his ill daughter. Aida's company improved the child's mood; she always brightened up when she saw Aida coming through the door and offered her some sweets she had at her bedside. Aida religiously visited the child every day and was happy when her little friend smiled and enjoyed her company. The sick girl loved Aida's pretty face, particularly her rosy cheeks, which she caressed gently with a soft handkerchief and compared to red, polished apples. Aida felt she did the child a lot of good. In later years she lost track of the landlord and his family but often thought of the girl and wondered how she was doing.

Aida was kept very busy but she also found time to roam around and enjoy walks in the forest that bordered on the farm and was extremely intriguing to the former city girl. She liked to feast her eyes on the colorful wild flowers that grew in the surrounding meadows in the spring, on the many varieties of mushrooms that sprung up after a rain and, from afar, watch deer slowly and cautiously making their way toward the nearby river for a drink. At night, while falling asleep and although very tired, she felt safe, happy, and content with her life.

Unfortunately, all this did not last very long. The year was 1899 and the situation in the districts of Moldavia and Wallachia deteriorated as friction between the Jews and the rest of the population grew and led to riots and pogroms.[1] The Jews were accused of causing economic problems and were also alienated because of the religious and linguistic differences between them and the masses. Aida was quite oblivious to the seriousness of the situation in the relative calm of the countryside. Yet one day, when a Jewish family was murdered in a nearby homestead, her aunt decided to flee before their lives were taken away from them. Aida was not feeling well at the time, somewhat weakened by a nagging fever that had plagued her for a few days, but there was no time to be lost. Her aunt quickly collected a few of their most valuable belongings and left the farm in the dark of night. They were assisted by a couple of gentile friends who put their own lives in danger trying to help them. Later, Aida did not recall very well what had happened; she remembered vaguely being dragged along some forest trails and tripping over some huge tree roots that were sticking out of the ground and whose outline could barely be seen in the darkness. Somebody carried her over a body of water and her clothes got completely soaked. Afterwards she shivered for hours in a ditch—where they had to wait before they could continue their escape—unable to warm up, with her teeth rattling continuously. It was summer time though and that, most probably, saved Aida from contracting and dying of pneumonia. She must have lost consciousness a few times since she could recall only isolated episodes. She remembered waking up in a cart pulled by a bull, covered with a rough blanket, and being comforted by her aunt who was begging her not to make any noise, and then, finally, the few days they spent at the port in Odessa waiting for the ship that would take them to a safe haven. They were going to sail for Argentina to join some relatives who had immigrated to the New World a few years earlier.

On board the large ship, Aida recovered completely. The sea breezes seemed to agree with her and quickly, within a few days, she regained most of her strength as well as the rosy color in her cheeks. The vessel was large but old and smelly. Aida hated the hot compartment she and her aunt were given in the bottom of the ship and spent as little time there as she could. The voyage was mostly uneventful, the weather fair, and she never felt seasick but rather invigorated by the vast ocean that spread out in front of her and the taste of salt that she sensed on her tongue each time she leaned over the rails and watched the waves splash against the side of the ship. The fresh air improved the appetite she had lost during her illness, although she disliked the cooked food served in the third class dining room. She felt satisfied when she could sneak out a big slice of rye bread spread with some butter and eat it while watching the limitless sea. She wished she could have some of the fruits she saw the first class passengers enjoying on deck, but did not give it much thought since she had always been used to simple fare. Her mood improved considerably when, within a few days of the start of the voyage, she found a secret place where she could sleep without being subjected to the foul air and constant, intense rocking motion on her bunk in the belly of the vessel. The upper decks had many elegant lounging chairs that were used by passengers of the first and second class, but the third class deck had only a few older ones that had been discarded in some places since they were not fancy anymore and needed new upholstery. Aida found refuge in a corner, on one of those large folding chairs. She brought the small pillow from her bunk bed and the thick blanket that had been distributed to the third class passengers and arranged them on the chair. She felt relieved not to be captive anymore to the noise and excessive heat the adjacent machinery room generated, and thus she slept peacefully on the deck without anybody noticing her. Or at least that is what she thought.

When she woke up one morning and removed the cover, which she thought was hiding her from sight, she discovered next to the folding chair, neatly wrapped in a white napkin, a beautiful apple that made her mouth water. She looked around, completely surprised, but could not see anybody. She carried the gift downstairs to her aunt's bunk to tell her about it and offered to share the apple with her. The aunt was as amazed as she was but did not want the apple, and so Aida enjoyed it all by herself, on her favorite deck, watching the color of the waves change from blue to dark green and purple, and dreaming of a happy future as the ship continued its voyage to the new world. Each morning when she woke up, Aida found a fresh fruit, usually an apple, neatly wrapped in a white napkin, next to her chair. She tried to stay awake in order to find out who was bringing her those lovely presents but she could never fight her drowsiness and slept soundly. And, thus, the days and nights passed, and they arrived at the port of Buenos Aires without Aida having been able to solve the mystery of the secret gift giver.

Her aunt did not lose any time when she arrived in Argentina and within a few weeks, with the help of kind-hearted relatives, was able to set up a small shop where she manufactured clothes and sold them. Aida stayed with her aunt and helped her with the sewing. One day a young man came into the little store and asked for her aunt. Aida looked at him and thought he seemed familiar but could not place him. The aunt and the young man had a talk in the back room and then the visitor left abruptly, looking pale and distressed, and, without glancing at Aida, placed next to her a nicely wrapped package. Aida hesitated only for a minute but then excitement took over and, when she opened the box, she found inside a couple of beautiful apples, wrapped in the same thin, elegant napkins as the ones on the ship. She went to look for her aunt, who had remained in the back of the store after the young man had left, and found her rather agitated. The older woman, who had a frown on her face, dismissed the question her niece asked and would not discuss it. Aida was very curious but, having been taught since childhood to be obedient and respectful towards the older members of her family, did not dare to confront her strict aunt. Only months later did she find out that the young man, who was the ship's doctor, had fallen in love with her. Being bashful and timid, he had not approached her on the ship but expressed his feelings with the gifts he placed every morning at the side of the reclining chair. However, he had been shrewd enough to find out her aunt's name and address in Buenos Aires and had come to see them to ask for permission to court Aida, with the intention of marrying her at a later date since she was still so very young. Aida never found out why her aunt had rejected him so quickly without even telling her. Pondering about it, she came to the conclusion that, although handsome and educated, with a promising future as a doctor, he was most probably not Jewish, and that must have been the main reason for the fateful decision. In any case, she did not attempt to bring it up and, since she had not been in love with the young man in the first place, forgot about it after a while. Small packages filled with fruits and sweets kept arriving at her address for some time whenever that ship docked in Buenos Aires. Aida, rather than boasting about it, often felt sorrow and pity for the young man who had so desperately fallen in love with an unknown girl with rosy cheeks.

Source Note

Based on an interview with Myriam Diner in Buenos Aires, March 2002. Aida Tenembaum was Myriam's maternal grandmother, an extraordinary person who lived until she was one hundred and two and left a strong impact on members of her family who cherish her memory.

Text Note

1. From 1835 to 1856, Moldavia and Wallachia, a region in south central Europe bordering Ukraine, was a protectorate of Russia. Anti-Semitism increased and Jews were not allowed to settle down in certain areas, practice certain professions, and citizenship was denied to them. After the Crimean War, in 1856, the situation improved but only native Jews were granted political rights. In 1878, when Romania became independent, non-citizen Jews could not hold public office, own land, or vote in Moldavia. Moldavia had been the center of Jewish life for many years—in 1899 there were close to 200,000 Jews living there—but emigration began to rise when conditions continued to deteriorate (*http://www.shtetlinks.jewishgen.org*).

The Artist

The *alfajores* were served on a beautiful tray with small cups of strong, fragrant coffee. Pepi, the lady of the house—tall, fragile, and with a friendly smile—asked the servant to place them on the long coffee table. "Alfajores," she said, "are Peruvian specialty cookies. It is true that you can find them in many South American countries, but the ones we make here are the very best. The butter, the ground almonds, and the caramel filling, in between two layers of crisp, golden brown rounds of scrumptious baked dough, make them irresistible."

Her husband, Armando, a retired dentist, was sitting on the sofa, surrounded by the many canvasses painted by Pepi. Art is Pepi's passion and her work adorns most of the walls in their house. They are mainly abstracts with outlines of people and objects: here one can see a trumpet, there a saxophone player, the profile of a face, the shadow a piece of furniture is casting . . . some paintings seem surrealistic, some impressionistic, a mixture of different styles that at times blend and sometimes do not in an amazing array of colors. The pictures are out of the ordinary, just like Pepi's name, which is actually her nickname, based on the character of a chambermaid found in Franz Kafka's "Castle," where she discovered it for the first time. She wants to make sure that it is not confused with the name of one of the old Pharos of Egypt or taken as a variant of Pepa; she wants to emphasize the connection to Kafka who is one of her favorite authors. Her real name is Rosalinda, which was given to her by her parents, who were immigrants from Romania.

Pepi knows only a few incidents from her parents' lives back in Europe before they settled down in the town of Trujillo in Peru. Her father, from whom she inherited her tall build, was a soldier in the Austro-Hungarian Empire during World War I and was always amazed that he had survived unlike many of his friends who had been killed by enemy fire. He did not escape completely unharmed, though, and his disability, since those days, made his life difficult for the rest of his days.

One evening, while his company was in the trenches and he was busy digging an additional foxhole, a grenade hit nearby; he heard the sound of the explosion mingled with the terrifying cry of wounded comrades and lost consciousness for a while. He thought he saw a large number of white, broken pieces of some substance floating in mid air, as if a whole set of porcelain cups had exploded. When he came to himself, he found that he was still in the foxhole, but covered with blood and with the body of a comrade on top of him. He managed to free himself and tried to help the other soldier but the man was already dead. He thought that the blood that covered him was the dead man's but, when the shock wore off somewhat, he felt an acute pain all over his face and realized that the blood was pouring out of his own mouth. He was sure that he was doomed. Nevertheless, at the field hospital, he was told that his essential organs were not damaged, as he had feared, just his mouth had been hit, and that after some healing process he would recover. However, things would be different from then on—all his teeth were gone, blown away by the explosion. His mouth had become an empty, sore pit. This situation weighed on him heavily and it led to an addiction to nicotine. He was a heavy smoker all his life.

Armando, the dentist, nods his head with compassion. He understands the misery of people who have to live toothless while still young and undergo various procedures to remedy, in many cases, a neglect of months or even years. The Jews seem to be more aware of the need for good dental care than the rest of the population in Peru, but then many of them are quite wealthy. Poor people cannot afford preventive treatments and that, unfortunately, leads to other serious diseases; yet it is ironic that people from abroad come to Peru to have their teeth taken care of since it is much cheaper than in other places. The maid brings another tray with more coffee and Pepi carefully moves aside a whole set of beautiful small boxes, of different sizes and materials, with elaborate carvings and engravings, that she has been collecting for years and likes to display. Just by chance, a gift from a friend had led to a lifetime hobby—a collection of extraordinary items—that complements Pepi's artistic tendencies.

Pepi smiles as she remembers an incident from her childhood in Trujillo. Very few Jews lived in that little town and they, like most inhabitants there, were very poor. The school was a terribly drab place where children sat on the floor because of a lack of chairs. They had to stand up each time they wanted to write something on the small desks that were provided. One day, lady luck smiled on them. Trucks that brought gasoline to town always delivered it in barrels that were enclosed in crates. When these containers were removed, the boxes were discarded. The teachers noticed and collected all the crates, brought them to school, and fixed them up so that the children could use them as little "chairs" and study more comfortably. Little Pepi sat on them until she was six years old.

Armando also has a special place in his heart for the town of Trujillo. Not only did he meet his beloved Pepi there, but he also remembers many of the local people who used to congregate, meet for a cup of coffee, and tell tales and jokes. One of his favorite folk anecdotes originates in Trujillo, although some Jews in Lima consider it their own. One day a Jewish merchant from Trujillo moved to Lima and settled down there. He became very rich; nevertheless, he was not of a generous nature but plain frugal and very careful with every penny he made. So stingy was he that he did not even allow himself to marry and have a family of his own, anxious not to share his fortune with anybody. However, he did at times have to entertain some fellow businessmen, yet found a way to economize on that, too. Any time he had a guest (and he did not have too many!), the maid was ordered that when asked to bring the main dish—which was usually fish (cheaper than meat!)—she should say, in a tearful voice, that the cat had eaten it. This happened over and over again, and each time the servant did as she was told. Once a very important dignitary came to visit the merchant and he wanted to make a good impression. He called the servant and told her to bring the fish. She began reciting, "Señor, the cat ate . . ." but the merchant stopped her and told her that it was different that time and she should bring the food as requested. The maid stood there unhappily and blurted out fearfully, "But, patron, this time the cat really ate the fish . . ."

Pepi and Armando have been very happy throughout their

marriage. They moved to Lima when they were still very young. Pepi studied chemistry for a while but her main interest has always been painting, and that is what she has pursued all her life. She has had some exhibitions but has no commercial knack for selling her pictures and, thus, she does it mainly for her own enjoyment. She has kept some friendships that started in Trujillo, not just with Jews but also gentiles. Anti-Semitism was never a big issue in their lives. It seems that they, as well as their neighbors, always followed the motto: "live and let live."

Source Note
Based on an interview with Rosalinda Loebl de Peck and Armando Peck in Lima, Peru, 2001.

Esther Solymosy

Esther was a little girl who years ago lived in a small village near the town of Miskolc in the north of Hungary, in the shadow of the Bukk Mountains. Ancient stone features of limestone, dolomite, and clay slate are abundant in that region. The Bukk area is well known for its glass-making workshops that originally manufactured much-needed window-panes. Later on, production of artistic blown glassware became quite prevalent with the arrival of workers from Slovakia and Poland who settled down in that part of the country and excelled in their craft. Some of these people were Jews who mingled with the population and initially lived in peace and understanding with the locals. In time, though, things changed and anti-Semitic sentiments became quite evident.

Esther had many friends among the children in the village. In the summer months they were free to roam around and enjoy the fresh air and singular beauty of the countryside. Esther's parents were observant Christians, peasants who owned a cottage and a small field in which they grew vegetables and grain that provided them with adequate food as well as a major source of income. Esther was the most cheerful of the five siblings and the only girl. Most of all she loved to dance, and her mother had created for her a beautiful outfit that consisted of a few layers of flowing, embroidered skirts and a simple white blouse. She wore long boots and her curly, black hair was gathered and decorated with a single flower. The costume was typically Hungarian and so were the folk dances in which Esther excelled. She was very graceful and her movements quite intricate. She could dance to the tune of one fiddle or to the sound of her own mother's voice. Esther's parents, as well as many of the inhabitants of the village, were reclusive people. To a certain extent they could have been considered sullen and dour but that might have been the way they expressed their loneliness over the centuries since their closest relatives were the faraway Finns and

Estonians. They might have felt that they never had much in common with the Slavs, their closest neighbors. The hardships of living and surviving in that little village were always difficult to bear. One could sense it in their mostly lamenting and melancholy melodies, which were hauntingly touching yet a source of their inner strength.

The Jews were considered foreigners; they had business contacts with the gentiles and had a decent relationship with them but there were no warm feelings or friendships lost. Most of them were Slovaks who had lived in Hungary for some time, mastered the language, and respected the habits and customs of the population. They kept to themselves and their religious practices always seemed strange and mysterious to the villagers. The Jews had a couple of minians and met every day and on holidays in one of the bigger houses they used as a synagogue for prayers and celebrations. Passover was the most difficult holiday to keep since they had to bake their own *matzah* and stop buying bread at the local bakery, which always puzzled the gentiles. The Jews readily explained it and also told them the story of Exodus, which the people already knew from the Bible. However, the locals never stopped being suspicious and believed that the Jews were up to something on their holidays, especially on Passover. It was, indeed, one year at Passover that a tragedy occurred.

It so happened that Esther had found a new friend among the Jews, a girl about her age by the name of Rivke, with whom she enjoyed spending the afternoons after school. They became very attached to each other and Esther liked to spend time at Rivke's home and eat some of the tasty foods her mother prepared. Esther's mother was not happy that the friendship between the two girls was becoming so strong but was too busy to worry about it. Rivke's parents, on the other hand, had only two children and welcomed Esther to their home. Rivke's mother told Esther the story of Purim and the Persian Queen Esther who had saved the Jews from impending disaster. Esther listened attentively and sighed with relief when the story had a good ending.

Passover and Easter fell on the same week that fateful year. Scores of visitors had arrived; the village was humming with relatives and friends as well as some vagrants who habitually came to the area to ask for free meals. Rivke joined Esther in the Easter celebrations and the typical customs of the Hungarian village. She got soaked as boys went around the village on horse carriages throwing buckets of water on any girl they saw in the street. She followed her friend who went around distributing painted eggs to the neighbors and even learned how to play some Easter melodies on the *cimbalom*—a stringed instrument—that one of Esther's brothers owned.

The day of the Seder, Rivke's mother was very busy and needed her daughter's help. When Esther came by to play with her friend and found Rivke immersed in the holiday preparations, she was disappointed and left to return home. She never got there and disappeared without a trace. Towards evening, Esther's worried mother came to Rivke's house calling her daughter's name. When she learned that Esther had left hours earlier, she summoned the father, the brothers, and some neighbors. They fanned out looking for the girl in every nook and corner of the village, as well as the outskirts. The search lasted all night and through the next day but they could not find her; seemingly she had vanished into thin air. The second day, toward nightfall, a shepherd coming home with his sheep noticed some dark substance on a formation of limestone in a deserted area that he passed on occasion. When he approached to check it out, he realized that it was quite a substantial amount of blood that had dried out and blackened in the sun. He reported it to the villagers and they all went running to the place. There was no doubt that it was human blood that they found all over the rocks but there was no sign of a body. They continued their desperate search for Esther for many weeks but she was never found. In time, they were forced to give up but the suspicion that had fallen on the Jews, particularly Rivke's family, because of the myth of Passover and the supposed need of blood to bake the matzah, weighed heavily on the Jews in the village. Some of them were beaten up; others were threatened and their property damaged. Within a few months an exodus from the village began, since most of the Jews felt compelled to find a safer place to live. A handful of families remained, among them Rivke's family. They felt miserable and desolate that Esther had disappeared and that they were suspected as the cause of her ill-fated demise, but they had no place to go. They hoped that, in time, things would improve, but the hostility never ceased and the lives of the remaining Jews became almost unbearable. Rivke grew up solemn and frightened, always remembering Esther who had been a beloved friend, the only one she had in the village. Rivke's mother was expecting another child and, toward the end of the pregnancy, became very big, as she was carrying twins. She avoided going into the village so as to escape the abuse and ridicule of the Christians. Children followed her wherever she went, mockingly chanting a rhyme that made her hair stand up:

> Ennek a zidovak de nagy hasa van,
> Talan a Solymosi Esther bene van!

The rhyme meant:

> What a big belly this Jew has,
> Perhaps Esther Solymosy is inside it!

Since they believed Jews needed blood to bake matzah, there was nobody in the village who did not agree that they had murdered Esther. Rivke tried to explain at school how matzah was made, and that the brown-reddish flakes on the surface were just the way baked goods came out sometimes because certain areas cooked faster than others. She even brought some buns from the village bakery to show that they too had discolorations of a similar kind. The teacher listened but her response was vague and disinterested and, tragically, no one was ready to admit that the myth about blood and matzah was just delirious nonsense. Time went by, things did change somewhat, but the proverb remained . . .

Source Note

Based on an interview with Maxine Lowy in Santiago, Chile, March 2002, and a proverb her father, Professor Lowy, mentioned to her in a letter. Professor Lowy recalled the tale his mother, Marishka, born in Miskolc, had told him about Esther Solymosy and the persecution of Jews in Hungary.

A Different Kind of Shtetl

It was not a village like Kasrilevke, Veribivka, or Boiberick, tiny shtetls in Eastern Europe immortalized by Mendele Mocher Sefarim and Shalom Aleichem.[1] The setting was different—the scenery, the weather, and, mainly, the Jews who lived there. They did not wear heavy kaftans and thick fur caps, nor did they spend most of their days in the synagogue; rather one could see them, with their sleeves rolled up, working in the fields—sowing, planting, or reaping, depending on the season—milking the cows, and breeding and riding horses with ease and confidence. Gone was the pallor and the yellowish complexion that had been so typical of them in the Old Country; their faces were red and sun burnt, their bodies muscular, and their hands full of calluses, hardened by the intense farming they were engaged in continuously. Some of them left as they were not able to cope with the rigors of harsh labor and other problems that arose, but those who remained, at least for a certain amount of time, experienced a rebirth and prospered. They learned to ride horses as the local *gauchos* did and acquired some of their habits and knowledge of the terrain. They became familiar with the forces of nature and were able to judge the onset of certain weather patterns thanks to the gift of observation based on experience but some-times also native superstition.

Palmar Yatay was one of the colonies indebted to Baron Hirsch for its existence.[2] It was far away from the suppression and the abuse the Jews had had to live with in the countries of their origin. At the begin-ning of the twentieth century many Jewish families arrived there with valises full of belongings and hearts full of hope. The Baron Hirsch foundation gave each person about two-hundred-and-fifty acres, which was not really much in Argentina since they had cows to graze in addi-tion to the cultivation of crops. Typically a family had thirty to forty head of cattle. They sold a few of them from time to time to the butcher and used the rest for milking. They also had poultry for consumption and a few horses for work as well as riding around the land. The colony was about fifteen kilometers from the town of Ubajay in the province of Entre Rios and got its name from the many beautiful Yatay palm trees that were abundant in the area.[3] From December to March, the Yatay palm was covered with dense yellow flowers that could be seen from afar and its fruits, small and hard, mingled with the blossoms well before the flowers withered and disappeared. The natives used the leaves to create a variety of baskets.

Faint memories of those days gone by still linger in the minds of some people who spent part of their childhood in Palmar Yatay. Two brothers, whose family had lived there for many years before the Depression in the 1930s, when their parents had to move to Buenos Aires in search of work, reminisce about those early days of their lives. Alberto, the younger, was a very small child when they lived in the colony and can recall only some flickers of images and events, which were, however, very significant in his young life. Teodoro, the older one, who began going to school in Ubajay, remembers more.

They lived in a farmhouse together with their paternal grandparents who had emigrated from Ukraine in 1908. Their maternal grandparents, who had come from England (but originated in Bessarabia), had arrived in Argentina around the same time and lived about three kilometers away, in another homestead. Regular school in the colony went only up to the seventh grade and the Jews were always very careful to supplement the standard education with their own. No matter how poor they were and how much in need or distress, the most crucial endeavor for the community was to have their synagogue and provide adequate learning for the children, and they were very successful in doing both. They were ardent keepers of tradition despite the fact that religion was not observed as rigorously as back in the little villages of Europe, where the majority of the Jews were orthodox. Alberto and Teodoro's father knew the Bible and Talmud extremely well, yet at times the holidays were celebrated in an abridged manner since it all depended on the workload and whether they could afford to take a day off. One exception was Yom Kippur, considered always the most sacred of all Jewish holidays, and, as such, observed meticulously according to the rules. Being Jewish, to most of them, meant that they should cherish their heritage, join the Zionist movement, and yearn for the creation of the State of Israel. Those were the main factors that kept the Jewish communities closely knit. In addition, the official religion of the country was Catholicism and, although they did not sense much discrimination on the surface, Jews found many doors closed and many opportunities undermined because of the plain fact that they were always regarded, either openly or secretly, as the killers of Christ. Thus, as it had been in Europe, they relied mainly on one another.

Alberto remembers that his father loved farming and was able to provide for his family as well as his own parents. He recalls the festive day when the cooperative bought a tractor for its members and how the families got together to celebrate on that occasion. He remembers Teodoro riding to school on a horse and their big police dog keeping him company while his brother was away. The dog was a good animal, beloved by the children and affectionate as well, yet they had to let go of him since he was not able to resist the urge to eat the chickens, which was something they could not afford. In the afternoons, children would congregate outside and play soccer or just sit around, and at times get into fights. The secular school Teodoro attended consisted of two rooms, each with three rows of benches, one grade per row for a total of six grades. A couple of teachers took turns teaching the lower and the upper grades. The children did not get any food except for a small roll and something to drink. The teachers, a husband and a wife, had inherited certain prejudices, which they passed on to their students without thinking too much. On one occasion, they mentioned that the Jews had murdered Christ and, on another, warned them not to spit since Jews did that and, thus, they would be labeled as Jews. Teodoro brought the information home, asking who was Christ, why did the Jews kill him, and what was the reason they spat so much? The next day his father went to see the teacher despite the fact that he could hardly afford to take the time off. He was a tall man, very imposing, and when he descended from his horse and entered the schoolyard, all the children were in awe. When he asked the teacher for an explanation, she denied the first accusation and also insisted that the boy had misheard when she had said *guanacos* and not Judios. The guanacos are relatives of the llamas that live in the Andes and they have a habit of rolling the food in their mouth into a little ball and aiming it at those who displease them. They always hit the target and it is very painful to the victim. Such was the teacher's poor excuse, but the children learned in that way what it meant to be Jewish and the father felt that he had to nip those kinds of anti-Semitic remarks in the bud. That was much easier in the colony than later on in the big city where the number of Jew-haters was large and harder to cope with. There were not too many gentiles around Palmar Yatay and the children did not have much contact with them except during planting and harvesting. The criollos,[4] as well as some gauchos,[5] were seasonal workers hired to help with the enormous amount of work the farmers had to handle. Life was very frugal but also rewarding in many ways; the children were not only exposed to nature but were also able to observe the habits and customs of other people.

Once Alberto was playing outside while his mother was very busy indoors. Being a toddler, everything in the world was new and interesting to him. He liked to explore and touch anything in sight. His mother had told him gently many times not to sit on the dirt. One day he saw many tiny red creatures marching in line on the soil; he followed them and sat down nearby to watch them. That was a big mistake that he remembered very well and never repeated. Those ants were the so called "sugar ants," only one sixteenth of an inch long, very fond of sweets but ready to consume voraciously anything eatable that came their way. They also excelled in warfare and were audacious warriors when needed. Alberto watched with fascination the happenings in the colony: how the ants loaded up on food for the winter and how they attacked another group of ants from a different colony that had invaded their boundaries. They fought fiercely, ripping off their enemies' bodies, and leaving piles of casualties on the ground. They also spurted out toxic chemicals that, in addition to the bites administered to

Alberto's tender anatomy, made him scream his head off and brought his mother frantically running out of the kitchen. The rash and the burning sensation subsided in time, but the memory of that really unpleasant experience prevailed and Alberto never ever again sat on the dirt. The ants were far more convincing than his mother and she enjoyed pointing that out. There were also many reptiles on the grounds of the farm, particularly snakes that appeared mostly during the time of plowing, some of which were dangerous. Alberto remembers his father killing one of those snakes with his belt.

There was one doctor and a pharmacy that served the colony. The people received information on healthcare and read, initially, the Yiddish newspapers and, later, also the Spanish publications that were sent from the capital and reached them twice a week. All the Jewish settlers knew how to read and write, and every home had articles on healthcare and agricultural issues; they were well informed. Once in a while, though, when in doubt, they consulted local curanderos—the spiritual healers or shamans, some of who had very good reputations.[6]

The settlers were very conscious of all the different customs and practices around them but were hardly influenced by them. Nevertheless, as much as they were self-contained and followed their own old habits, Argentinean culture penetrated into their everyday lives, and that was obvious and consistent in many aspects of their existence and dominant in artistic endeavors such as their new songs. They joked about it and accepted it as part of their new way of life. An immigrant from Lithuania, singing in broken Argentinean Spanish, boasts of learning the difficult Castilian language in one month and attributes that achievement to the fact that he had been eating the popular Argentinean boiled beef three times a day, which must have been a miraculous potion.[7] A young man sings in Yiddish about the joy of being able to date a young girl, so unlike in the Old Country; however, the Jewish mother is still there to protect the virtue of her daughter and he has to be aware she might attack him with a broom when he walks her daughter home. And so he croons humorously about his woes:

Ij gei bainajt in cine	*I go to the movies at night*
A meidel ven ij zei	*When I see a girl*
Ij bin in Argentine	*I'm in Argentina*
Un ij gei mit ir aheim	*And I walk her home.*
Ij loz ihr geien aintkegen	*I let her walk in front of me*
Un ij gei bai di vant	*And I walk by the wall*
Vail di mame shteit in toier	*Because the mother stands at the door*
Mit a beizem in'm hant !	*With a broom in her hand!*
Oy ojo! Oy mucho ojo!	*Beware!*
Oy ojo, oy mucho ojo,	*Beware!*
Vail ver s'hot ojo,	*Because he who is aware*
Hot mazel brojo,	*Is blessed with luck*
Un ver es hot nisht	*And he who isn't*
Is nisht far mihr gedajt	*It isn't for me to worry about.*[8]

All in all life was not always a bowl of cherries but humor never failed to enhance it.

Source Notes

Based on an interview with Alberto Socolovsky, recorded by Hana Josephy in April 2001. Additional information provided by Alberto and Teodoro Socolovky in March 2003. Both Alberto and Teodoro Socolovsky are engineers; they spent their childhood and young adult years in Argentina. Teodoro and his family live in Israel and Alberto resides with his family in the United States.

Songs are by Hevel Katz; transliteration and translation provided by Alberto Socolovsky. Hevel Katz was a Yiddish comic singer who wrote and sang humorous songs in Yiddish and Castellano in Argentina during the 1930s.

Text Notes

1. Mendele Mocher Sefarim (Shalom Yaacov Abramovitz, 1836–1917) and Shalom Aleichem (Shalom Rabinowitz, 1859–1916) are regarded as the fathers of modern Yiddish literature.

2. Please see "Ode to a Dead Son" for more information on Baron de Hirsch.

3. *Yatai* in the Guarani tribe language means small hard fruit: yua—small fruit; ata—hard. Species of this hardy and wind tolerant palm tree grow in Brazil, Paraguay, Uruguay, and in the northwest provinces of Argentina.

4. The criollos are natives—part Indian, part Spanish—that suffer from extreme poverty and find seasonal work every year whenever possible. They have their own habits and customs, most of which have evolved from their modest surroundings. Their habitat generally consists of simple wooden shacks that have, at times, plastic curtains or streamers instead of doors and, thus, visitors cannot just knock on the door but have to clap hands to announce their presence. They are very meticulous and have the habit (like many Argentineans) of sweeping the area outside the door before cleaning the inside of their homes. They do it with a broom regardless of whether it is a sidewalk, a driveway, or a dirt area. The women like to decorate and adorn their flower gardens with painted shells from huge snails that abound in Argentina.

5. The gauchos are colorful people. They are not just cowboys and hardy men but have their own folklore that shows itself not only in their storytelling and their songs but also in their attire. The typical, elegantly dressed gaucho would wear a leather hat on top of a handkerchief; both items are meant mainly to protect him from the sun, the wind, and his sweat. From their leather vest and ample sleeved shirts to their wide woven ponchos and tall boots, they are a sight to behold. Some of them wear *chiripas*, which is a light fabric worn between the legs like some sort of inner trousers. Their garments are only a part of the impressive image they create.

6. Curanderos—shamans or faith healers—provided interesting and, at times, very useful information about their traditional way of healing that had to do with herbal treatments as well as rituals. The curanderos believed that many of the illnesses are caused by emotional and psychological sources. They also regarded the powerful forces of nature as causes of certain diseases. Sometimes modern remedies failed to offer an appropriate treatment for the ill. Herbal remedies could then be used as a substitute, as a fusion of traditional and popular medicine, particularly in far-removed communities.

7. "El Inmigrante Litvak" ("The Immigrant from Lithuania") in broken Argentinean Spanish.

Nacido yo soy un lituano	*I'm a native Litvak*
Nacido yo soy un lituano	*I'm a native Litvak*
Hace año y mes	*I've been in the country*
Que estoy en país	*A year and one month,*
Y ya se hablar castellano.	*And I can already speak Castilian*

Castellano aprendí muy ligero	*I learned Castilian very fast*
Castellano aprendí muy ligero	*I learned Castilian very fast*
Por que yo sabía	*Because I knew*
Tres veces por día	*Three times a day*
Hay que comer buen puchero	*To eat boiled beef.*

8. The first two stanzas, plus refrain of "Oy ojo!" ("Beware"); the Yiddish is transliterated using Spanish alphabet. For example: "ij" for "I" instead of "ich"; "gei" for "walk" instead of "gay." The refrain uses the Argentinism "ojo" (eye) for "beware!" or "watch out!"

Neckties, Anyone?

The two brothers looked out of the window at the passing landscape as the train was winding its way from the city of Santiago into the countryside. The older one began reading a newspaper; the younger, about eight years his junior, was watching the swift change of scenery as the locomotive picked up speed. Two suitcases, a big one and a smaller one, were stacked one on top of the other. They were old, their weatherworn leather spotted and pale, and held tightly by a belt of some sort to prevent the locks from popping open. It was obvious that they had been used heavily in the past and that they would not last much longer, no matter what their content was or how carefully they were handled. When, around a bend, a small town appeared as if from nowhere, the brothers got up, waited for the train to pull into the tiny station, and, picking up their suitcases, jumped off even before it came to a full stop. Both brothers were helping their father to make a living for the family. They were peddlers and traveled to many places around Santiago to sell the merchandise their father manufactured in a small workshop in the city.[1]

Their old man was a tie-maker. He was a merchant and an artist as well. In his small shop he had a large number of different kinds of materials, ranging from the very cheap to the most expensive—some cottons, wools, and silks, and some fabrics that served mainly as lining for the ties he created. He did the measuring, cutting, and sewing with the help of a couple of people to whom he taught his craft. His sons were asked to help only temporarily with the sales since the father wanted them to get a better education than he had received and be able to succeed in the world. The old man loved his occupation and was very knowledgeable in all related matters, particularly talented and way ahead of the times when it came to marketing. He prepared colorful flyers that advertised his merchandise, describing the ties, the fabrics, the different colors, designs, and styles, and even offered discounts if a person purchased at least two. More than anything else, he loved to tell people the story of how the tie, *la cravata,*had come into being. He would sit down on a bench and, holding one of the ties in his hands, turn into a historian. The tie to him was not just a large band of fabric that men tied around their necks; it was a fashion statement that went way back in time. He knew about the kings of Egypt and the emperors of China who wore rectangular pieces of fabric around their necks, hanging loose on their shoulders as a status symbol. He pointed out that the tie served not only as an object of decoration but that there were also health benefits associated with it. In the days of the glorious Roman Empire, men who wore some sort of neckwear were mainly the orators who wanted to protect their vocal cords. He told the story of how the vain Louis XIV was fascinated by the colorful handkerchiefs that officers of a regiment from Croatia tied around their necks. Soon there were Royal cravattes (the name was derived from the word Croat) fashioned only for His Majesty. The tie-maker finished his little lecture by stating that from the seventeenth century on the necktie became well known all over the world, with some ups and down in popularity, but that he believed it would never stop being an indicator of great personal taste, if not social status.

The brothers always separated at a fork in a road or at a street corner, and each went his way, knocking on the doors of the houses in the area. They wore nice suits with a colorful tie wrapped once around their neck and looped into a perfect knot. They addressed the prospective customers with a broad smile, handing them an envelope into which they had inserted a flyer and two neckties of different styles and colors. They presented their merchandise politely, without putting any pressure but rather by offering to leave the ties with the customer to look at, try on, and decide if he wanted them or not. They would come back in a couple of days to see what had been decided, hoping for a sale, but there were no ties attached, so to speak! Sometimes they were invited in and the lady of the house served them coffee and some baked goods. They opened up their suitcases and laid out about two- or three-dozen neckties, explaining the different styles and fabrics. They would ask the customer to feel the fabric and teach them to recognize the type of material each tie was made of. A rougher texture, for example, meant that the necktie, although beautifully cut and stitched, was made of a silk of inferior quality and therefore sold for less. They explained how a tie was cut from a single square piece of material and folded seven times in order to give the necktie the proper resilience. They showed how the lining gave the tie its fullness and that the best were lined with wool. Their honest approach and unique way of selling brought them good business. People seemed to appreciate it and enjoyed their presentations, which were as colorful as the ties themselves. The customers mostly responded very well; they never cheated and either returned the ties in perfect condition or paid for them. There were hardly any incidents of the ties being stained or torn. Ties in those days, in the 1930s and 1940s, were good business. It was a cultural thing; almost everybody wore a tie—if not during the week, on Saturdays and Sundays for sure. People regarded them as a worthwhile, inherited tradition, an object of aesthetic value that gave them a sense of luxury and formal elegance.

When the tie-maker retired, he moved out of Santiago to a valley, about four hundred and twenty kilometers away, where he spent the rest of his life. The younger brother went into the study of law in his twenties but continued for some time to be a traveling salesman. He found the income to be very useful and also felt compelled to assist a Jewish peddler who had become an associate. This older man was not able to carry the heavy suitcases and so they traveled together. He has not dealt with neckties for many years since becoming a lawyer, but still has a soft spot in his heart for them and follows the new innovations in design and fabrics. He thinks of his old man often, especially when he visits the shop that his father had established. His older brother and his in-laws, who no longer exclusively sell ties, now own the place.

Source Note

Based on an interview with Washington Domb in Santiago, Chile, March 2002.
http://www.shop-usa.info/TIE.History/tie
http://www.astiesgoby.com
http://www.getcustoms.com/articles/ties

Text Note

1. There is a multitude of stories about Jewish peddlers in Latin America; most of them dealt with different types of merchandise; they did not necessarily specialize in one kind nor did they manufacture any particular item. There were a few exceptions, such as this tie-maker, the jewelry salesman (see *The Survivor*), and a Jew in the town of Temuco who, like the famous Mendele Mocher Sefarim in Eastern Europe, sold only books. The peddler in Temuco was the grandfather of Guillermo Preminger, an engineer who resides in Santiago. However, unlike Mendele, this man sold all kinds of books to Jews and gentiles alike in order to make ends meet. His wife, Frida, started a business that became the first elegant boutique for ladies in that town. The name of the shop was "Carlotta" and it was well known for its owner's refined taste. The *semaneros* were peddlers who offered installment plans to those who could not pay in full and came each week to collect the amount owed.

Albertito

Albertito existed only in the grandfather's mind but this character, a small Jewish boy, became, over time, a member of the family, and Zaideh himself believed that he was not just a figment of his imagination but a real, living, breathing kid. Zaideh had arrived in Buenos Aires in 1931 from Poland as a young man and had labored very hard to support his family with very little time left to devote to his children. As years went by, life became somewhat easier and, when grandchildren came along, he felt blessed and anxious to pass on to them the heritage he had not been able to share with his children. This legacy was not tangible; it was more than just love, tradition, and memories; it was a piece of his heart—fragments of his own childhood in a faraway country where life for the Jews had been harsh. Yet he did not want to tell them tales of suffering and woe; he wanted to entertain them and keep them happy and cheerful and, so, thanks to his storytelling talent and vivid imagination, he was able to combine the old with the new and create some very unique stories that nobody had ever heard before.

Zaideh was a man of average height who never lost the mane of thick, white hair that framed his face and enhanced the intense spark in his luminous eyes. They always shone brightly, particularly when he came up with a new idea for a story or when he watched his grandchildren sitting breathlessly at his side, listening to the tales.

"So," they used to ask, "is Albertito going to do something special today? Is he up to something?" And Zaideh, the grandfather, would smile a little and pretend that he did not know who Albertito was. "You mean Motke?" he would ask innocently.

"No, no," cried the children, "Albertito!"

"Oh, you mean, Motke, the little Polish boy who came to Argentina! Oh, oh, oh, yes, I have a story for you!"

And Zaideh began telling them a tale in perfect Spanish but with

a rather heavy Yiddish accent he had never been able to lose. He had
mastered Spanish quickly by attending night school upon his arrival in
Buenos Aires and gained complete command of the language that he
was very proud of. However, he also loved to insert Yiddish words in
his narratives and never forgot the Polish that was his mother tongue.

"Well," he would start, "Albertito, as you know, was a little boy who
lived in a small village. His mother was always busy taking care of their
large family and, since his father spent a lot of time praying in the synagogue, Albertito tried to be of help. Every day after he came back from
school, he went out into the field to look for their two goats that were grazing in the meadow and had to be brought home. The goats were siblings,
you see, quite young, and cared very much for each other and, most of all,
they loved Albertito. Albertito played with them, caressed them, talked to
them, and the three of them were quite a happy bunch. One summer afternoon, Albertito did not see the goats grazing in their usual place and got
worried when they did not respond to his call. He began following a
narrow path and, after a while, came to an abandoned well. He looked into
the depths of the pit and thought he saw something shiny down there.
What could it be? he pondered. He leaned over carefully but still could not
make out what it was. He kneeled and bent further down, then suddenly
lost his balance and, with a frightening scream, fell into the deep well.
Luckily he landed on something soft and realized that it was a heap of
grass. It had been piled up there for sometime, turned yellow, and the light
of the sun from above had made it sparkle and, unfortunately, it was not
the golden treasure he had imagined it to be. He began yelling for help, but
to no avail, and so after a while, feeling very tired, he gave up. The well was
quite far from the house and dusk was setting in and, although it was a big
and wide pit, he was worried that his family would not be able to find him
before morning. He felt very scared thinking that he might have to spend
the night inside the well. Suddenly he heard the sound of fluttering wings
and to his total amazement saw one of his goat friends hovering over the
pit. He realized he was not dreaming and that the goats had hidden wings
which he had never seen before. One of them descended slowly into the
well and Albertito grabbed her legs and held on with all his might. Before

he knew it, he was sitting on the grass outside the well and his two friends were next to him, licking his face. Oh, yes, they were not dogs, true, but when no one was around they showed their affection to Albertito just the way a dog would. Their wings were gone and no matter how meticulously Albertito searched for them, he could not find them anywhere on their bodies. Finally, he decided not to tell anybody about his adventure since nobody would believe that it had really happened and, thus, kept it a secret just between him and his goat friends. Never again did he go too close to open wells or pits, just in case the wings would not reappear on the goats and he would be in real trouble if he fell in again."

The grandchildren sighed a sigh of great relief that Albertito had been rescued.

"Did Albertito have any other unusual pets?" asked one of them.

"Let me see," answered Zaideh and closed his eyes half way, trying to look pensive. "Oh, yes," he said after a while, "Indeed he had. There was a multicolored rooster that lived in the backyard, yet he was very grim since Albertito's mother always paid attention to the hens that laid eggs but barely seemed to notice him. Actually, she disliked him a lot, mainly because he used to call out in the wee hours of the night, waking up the small children from their slumber as well as robbing the adults of their badly needed sleep. Albertito felt sorry for him and, at times, hosed him down with a gentle stream of water—since, most probably out of sheer desperation, the rooster used to wallow in mud, which did not improve his looks or his temper. He was a strange bird but very intelligent. He liked to listen to people's conversations and learned a few words in Yiddish. He kept the knowledge to himself for a long time till one evening when Albertito's father came home. The rooster was perched on a tree branch and, when he saw the master coming towards the house, he shrieked in a very clear voice, 'Tate alte schmate, Tate alte schmate!'— meaning 'Daddy is an old rag, Daddy is an old rag!'"

The angry farmer took a broom and chased the rooster out of the yard, and it might have been the end of the loud-mouthed bird had he not found refuge behind one of the chicken's cages. Albertito never found out whether the rooster knew more than just those three words in Yiddish and wondered how he learned them. He always had the suspicion that the rooster was actually a lost parrot from Iguazu who had, because of some misfortune, ended up on the farm and was doomed to live in disguise all his life.

Soccer was Zaideh's passion; it had been his favorite pastime in the Old Country and he was as enthusiastic as most Argentineans in his great attachment to the game. His grandchildren loved soccer as well. When asked how he played ball when he was young, Zaideh described his experiences in great detail. Back in those days, in the shtetl, the boys did not have a soccer field nor did they have goal posts. They played in any open area that was available; sometimes they did not even have a proper ball, just something to throw around, a "ball" made out of pieces of torn towels tied together or even an old pumpkin that had hardened and could be kicked around for a while before breaking up. Most of all, he amazed the children by telling them that, since they did not have goal posts, they used two cows instead. One of their black cows stood at one end of the field while at the other end they positioned a white cow, and the little kids played soccer in the pasture in between the two "posts"—it was perfect! The children listened with open mouths and asked whether the cows stayed there for any length of time; surely they must have walked away, but Zaideh, with his eyes twinkling, reassured them that the two animals stood there happily and served as goal posts through the entire game.

Zaideh died at the age of seventy and his family has missed him terribly since then. His "Albertito Tales"—and there were many of them—live on, though, and will be told and retold from one generation to another. He might even be listening to the new renditions, assuming, of course, that he is not too busy playing soccer in the heavenly fields, chasing two stubborn cows that will not stay in one place and wait patiently till the game has ended.

Source Note

Based on an interview with Anna Tarnaruder in Buenos Aires, March 2002. Anna is a librarian at the Seminario Rabinico and a relative of Hana Dukas, a dear friend of the author, who lives in Israel.

The Rabbi's Tomb

*T*he heat is oppressive in the town of Manaus that lies in the heart of the Amazon basin. It is extremely sultry every day of the year despite the heavy rainfall that allows, at times, a slight respite from the sticky sensation that the climate creates and cleanses the dust from the multitude of graves in the Sao Joao Batista Cemetery. Thus, the whitewashed tomb of Rabbi Shalom Imanuel Muyal glistens each time the downpour stops and the radiant sunrays polish the metal railing around it and enhance the Hebrew characters and the Star of David engraved on the headstone. It is a Christian graveyard but the great rabbi was buried there, about hundred years ago, since a Jewish burial site did not exist in those days. Yet, no person in the vast cemetery has the fame or the respect that surrounds that particular tomb which is visited even more by Christians than by Jews.[1]

In his lifetime the rabbi had been a devoted teacher and guide to the small community of Jews that had found their way into the Amazonia. Most of the members of his congregation originated from Morocco, where they enjoyed a temporary sanctuary after the expulsions from Spain and Portugal in the fifteenth and sixteenth centuries. There they became an important factor in the local economy, but when times became hard again, and they had to look for another haven, many of them ended up on the shores of Brazil, in Belém, at the gateway to the Amazon. Being mostly poor merchants and peddlers, they decided to look for fortune in the vast territory of the tropical jungle. During those two hundred years of Jewish history in Manaus, some of the Jewish merchants became rich thanks to the treasures they found in the Amazon, such as rubber and extracts from different trees that were made into intoxicating perfumes. Most of them, though, remained poor and those that lived there during the times of Rabbi Muyal found life-saving support and strength in his teachings and guidance. The rabbi tried to help the people in his community as much as he could, and it is believed that he even traveled to the Holy Land in search of assistance, both spiritual as well as material, for his impoverished congregation. The tales about the rabbi have passed from one generation to another: some told by *chachamim*, the wise men of the community, some surviving as anecdotes and sayings, yet all wrapped in mystery. He was remembered fondly for his devotion to the sacred Jewish holidays and, in particular, to the holiday of Mimouna, which, according to old Moroccan Jewish custom, follows Passover.[2] Many years went by and people continued to rely on his wisdom, and Jews, as well as Christians, felt the utmost respect for him that bordered almost on worship.

In those times various diseases, some more serious than others, often plagued the people of the Amazon. It so happened that one day the rabbi fell ill; it is not known whether he had a family, but when the disease struck, he was already an old, lonely man, weak and with a very low immunity. He had felt very tired for a couple of days and struggled with a fever, but soon enough he was not able to stand on his feet. The housekeeper found him delirious and incoherent, talking loudly in a language she did not understand. The rabbi's modest dwelling was exposed to the high humidity of the area; it was not built in a way that would allow cooling breezes to enter the rooms and facilitate circulation, yet insects and infecting mosquitoes could easily penetrate through the windows that had no screens or any other protection. Soon enough the word was out that the rabbi was very sick with some horrible disease and, despite the great regard people had for him, nobody dared to come near his home except for Florzinha, his loyal servant, who would not leave under any circumstances. The natives were familiar with epidemics that had been brought to the Amazon by white men. When the word went out that the rabbi had turned yellow and was in great pain and vomiting blood, they knew that his end was near. The rabbi had contracted Yellow Fever and, since there was no known treatment, most people died within a short period of time.[3]

Florzinha was a native Caboclo, whose people had dwelt in the jungles for many generations, and used the medicinal knowledge she had learned from the shamans of her tribe.[4] She rowed her canoe to a magical site outside of Manaus known as Solimoes, where the dark streams of the Rio Negro meet the brown waves of the Amazon, and collected some water at that very confluence. She boiled down the Ayahuasca, the "vine of the soul," and some other plants and applied the concoction to the body of the feverish rabbi. She gathered fruit from the Cupuacu tree that grew outdoors and, mashing the nutritious pulp, tried to feed the weak rabbi to help him fight the disease.[5] The unusual aroma that the fruit emitted was supposed to help reinforce the rabbi's weakened immune system. Despite all her efforts, the rabbi died within a few days and nobody would come to wash the cadaver and help her carry the body to the burial place. Florzinha herself had not been well preceding the rabbi's illness; she had suffered from a woman's ailment and was wasting away, with her skin covered in a mantle of a red, spreading rash. That was the additional reason why nobody braved to come near the rabbi's home. The fears of disease and death were stronger than the feeling of awe the people felt for the rabbi. Florzinha remembered the rituals the rabbi had performed in his lifetime and the way the Jews dealt with their dead. She cleansed the ravaged body of the rabbi and wrapped it in white linen. He had always been a small man and the illness had shrunk his body to the size of a child's. This made it easier for Florzinha to place him on a cart and push it all the way to the cemetery. There she dug a grave and buried him.

A few days after the rabbi's demise, Florzinha completely recovered from her illness, her rash disappeared, and so did all the other symptoms that had made life difficult and painful for her. People thought it was a miracle and the word spread that not only had her health been restored, but that she had also been bestowed with some magical powers that had been transmitted from the rabbi to her. From that day on, she became a healer and people flocked to her house in search of help.[6] Yet, more than anything else, they believed that it was the rabbi who was the real saint and the true story of his life and death became a legend that grew over time.

In 1928, when the Jewish community in Manaus was able to purchase a piece of land and consecrate it as their burial site, they wanted to transfer the remains of the rabbi to a place of honor in their own graveyard. However, the objection from the Christian population was so intense that they did not do it at the end, accepting the fact that the rabbi belonged to all the people of Manaus and, as such, could be worshipped where he had been buried in the first place. It is not easy to find the rabbi's tomb among the countless graves of the cemetery. It is very crowded and the paths are very narrow; yet once one reaches the tomb nestled among thousands of crosses that fill the graveyard, it is not just the Star of David and the Hebrew inscription that catch one's eye but the array of pebbles that have been placed on his grave over the years, as the Jewish custom requires, by Jews and non Jews alike. The thankful people, who believed he had helped them even from the grave, placed small, engraved plaques all around his resting-place, expressing their gratitude.

There is no doubt that Rabbi Muyal's grave is a timeless treasure of the Jewish community in Manaus but his heritage is not the only prize that the congregation has been blessed with. A Torah scroll that is over 400 years old has its place of honor in the Aron Hakodesh—the Sanctum—of the synagogue. It is opened only on the High Holidays and extreme care is taken so that the parchment, which is very brittle, does not deteriorate even more. The frail Torah goes back to the golden days of Jewish life in Portugal and its history, as well as its voyage across the seas until it reached Manaus, is shrouded in the past. A certain wise man by the name of Yaacob Azulay, who was the spiritual leader of the congregation for over five decades, deemed that many lives had been lost by those who protected the sacred scroll from destruction and that it reached Manaus hidden in the suitcase of a Jew who had initially come from Morocco to the coastal town of Belém. The people believe that the scroll has no magical powers; it is, nevertheless, a talisman they guard with great love and pride, an additional legacy they carry in their hearts.

Source Note

Based on interviews with Dr. Isaac Dahan and Jorge Bentes in Manaus, March 2002. Dr. Dahan is a medic who also served as the President, Hazan, and Shaliach Tsibur of the congregation in Manaus. Jorge Bentes is a consultant to the Ministry of Haciendas.

Text Notes

1. Cemeteries have always been a basic necessity for every Jewish community, including those in Morocco. Graves of "saints," rabbis, or *Tzaddikim* (righteous men) were recognized in many places. The stories about them varied; some were about individuals who had lived there during the time of the storytellers and others were tales about visitors who possessed special powers and had died during their stay in a particular place. In Morocco, congregations organized annual pilgrimages to the graves of certain "saints." These usually took place on the anniversary of their death, on their *hillula*. The tomb of the holy man had a specific structure built over it to distinguish it from other graves. This mystical tradition gave congregations a sense of togetherness and also created, in Morocco, a feeling of solidarity with their Muslims neighbors who have similar customs pertaining to pilgrimages to their holy places (*http://www.mondeber-ber.com/juifs/mellahs.htm*). The Amazonian Jews treasure this tradition. The congregation in Manaus regards Rabbi Muyal's grave as a *Nachala—a sacred ground of their own*—and every year during the *Yamim Noraim*—the High Holidays—they have a special ceremony in his honor, after which they visit his grave to pay their respects.

2. Mimouna is an ancient Moroccan Jewish custom of celebrating the day that follows Passover. It symbolizes the return, the reintegration of the Jews into society, after eight days of restricted meals. People set out to friends' homes bringing offerings of food not allowed during the eight days of Passover, including honey and milk in honor of Eretz Israel, and fish dishes, which symbolize prosperity. They walk from one home to another and sing:

> Yach, yach Mimouna,
> Yach Shalom,
> Yach Raba! (*Raba*—from the Hebrew meaning plenty)

The *yach* is an onomatopoeic expression of joy and happiness. The language used by the Manaus Jews is *Haketiah,* a mixture of Arabic, Hebrew, and Spanish, which was used by many Jews who lived in Morocco, and originated in Spain. It is mainly used orally as an every day language. Benedictions are sung in Ladino. The name of the holiday—Mimouna—has no accurate explanation—something to do with the father of Maimonides, Josef Ben Maimon, who had a wonderful relationship with his Muslim neighbors and was admired for that. The Muslims respected the festival of Mimouna and even participated by bringing food and gifts to their Jewish neighbors. (Comments – Dr. I. Dahan)

3. Yellow fever is a viral disease that has caused large epidemics in Africa and in the Americas stretching back about 400 years. It affects the liver, which cannot purify the blood anymore, and is called yellow because of the jaundice that some patients develop as a result of the liver malfunction. It killed thousands of Indians along the Amazon during the European explorations since 1615, surpassing at times the numbers of smallpox and malaria victims. In the tropical jungles wild mosquitoes that carry this virus infect monkeys and humans. An effective vaccine was found about sixty years ago but there is still no specific treatment for the disease except to keep the patient comfortable and, mainly, prevent dehydration.

4. Caboclo are inhabitants of the Amazonia. They are the descendants of mixed parents, indigenous Amazonians, as well as many different groups that came there mainly during the rubber rush. They were Brazilians from the Northeast, Portuguese, Bolivians, Peruvians, Jews, and others. The Caboclo learned from all these people and serve as a bridge between different cultures, but they are mostly very poor, uneducated, live a life of abandonment, and many times drift back in time and follow the habits and ways of the indigenous people of the Amazon. See Francisco Ritta Bernardino, *Emociones Amazonicas* (Manaus, Brazil: Photoamazonica, 1998).

5. Cupuacu (Cupuassu) is a small to medium tree that grows in the rainforest. It belongs to the chocolate family and can reach up to twenty meters in height. Cupuacu fruit has been a primary food source in the rainforest for indigenous tribes and animals alike. The fruit is about the size of a cantaloupe and has a creamy exotic tasting pulp. The pulp occupies approximately one-third of the fruit and is used throughout Brazil and Peru to make fresh juice, ice cream, jam, and tarts (*http://www.rain-tree.com/cupuasu.htm*).

6. Florzinha – The story of the courageous, compassionate woman who was the rabbi's servant is very obscure. After the rabbi's death she was able to heal any disease with her touch, and it was all attributed to the blessing of the rabbi she had served so faithfully. It is said that it is her great-grandson, Samuel, who serves nowadays as the Shammash at the synagogue.

The Boat Ride

It was pitch dark that night. The moon was hidden behind dense, black clouds and even the light of the brightest stars could not penetrate the thick blanket that divided the earth and the firmament. The river was calm and the waves were placid, as if the gloomy, impenetrable sky made them sluggish and sleepy. A small group of people was standing very still at one end of a narrow dock. They were all dressed in bleak clothes, hoping to merge with the scenery and not attract attention, yet there was a feeling of tension and unrest in the air. These people were Jews from Russia who had survived the horrors of the Holocaust and arrived a few days earlier in Montevideo thanks to the help of relatives who lived in Argentina. It was 1946 and the Peronist government, which had been elected the previous year, did not permit Jews to enter Argentina. The only way they could get in was to travel to Uruguay, Paraguay, or Bolivia and make it illegally from there. They had managed to travel from Montevideo to Salto, a city in northwestern Uruguay, on the Uruguay River, opposite Concordia in Argentina that was their initial destination.

The two men and two women were breathing quietly and almost immobile. One of the women held a tiny child in her arms that was all bundled up in a blanket and asleep. It was close to midnight when a small, blunt-bowed, slender-hulled sailing boat slipped into the dock and a man on board flashed a dim light three consecutive times. They had their flashlight ready and when they signaled back, the competent sailor eased the boat into the dock and attached a rope to one of the poles. He motioned to them to get in and helped each of the women while the men quickly tossed in a few suitcases they had stacked one on top of the other. The mother carefully sat down on one of the wooden benches and noticed with panic that there was some water on the floor of the boat. It looked fragile and leaky, and she prayed it would be safe for them to reach the other bank of the river; there was no other way out. The sailor was old and looked experienced and she had to trust the people in Montevideo who had helped them with the connection and to whom they had given most of their savings to facilitate the crossing. The sailor noticed her uneasiness and whispered a few sentences in Spanish that she did not understand. Later on she recalled a few words the old man had said and realized that he had tried to remove her fears by telling her that it was not difficult to navigate the lower river, where they were, since only its upper course was hazardous due to the Salto Grande Waterfalls.

The vessel took off almost with no sound and the sailor rowed slowly out into the main stream of the river. However, it was a really difficult effort for the old man since the wind started blowing against them. The baby woke up and let out a scream. The mother quickly tried to calm her down and inserted a small handkerchief into her mouth when she would not stop weeping. There was no pacifier available and that was the best thing she could do. They were terrified that the little girl's cries might disclose their location as they were still very near the shore. After a while, the child calmed down and fell asleep again and the boat moved smoothly down the river. The sailor unpacked a brown bag and offered them some food. He said quietly "chivito" and they knew he was offering them a popular Uruguayan sandwich filled with slices of meat, lettuce, and egg. They thanked him but refused since they were too nervous to even think about nourishment. Suddenly a few drops of rain fell on the passengers and it increased steadily as they continued to sail. The drizzly spells did not stop and the calm was abruptly broken by a strong wind, chilly and violent. The mother covered the child with a small tarp the sailor had provided and kept praying for safety. She was terrified and lost track of time. When they finally arrived safe and sound at the Argentinean shore, she felt, just as the others did, as if they had crossed the largest body of water and reached the ends of the world.

After a day in Concordia, located in the north of the province of Entre Rios, along the western banks of the Uruguay River, they boarded the train for Buenos Aires. They barely made it to the station on time since the people who aided them in Concordia were afraid to take them to the terminal and, instead, only provided general instructions on how to get there. Once aboard, they found some seats and felt a great relief when the train pulled out of the station. The city of Concordia is approximately four hundred and thirty eight kilometers from the capital and they endured a long ride trying to be as unnoticed as possible. Their friends in Concordia had given them a few local magazines that they held in front of them, pretending to read although they did not know Spanish at all. It gave them a false sense of safety hiding behind the papers; they were not aware that it actually attracted some attention despite the fact that they traveled during the night and most people on the train were either asleep or dozing off.

Their arrival at the main terminal in Buenos Aires was quite different, at first, from what they had envisioned. The danger of being caught was too tangible and, when they disembarked, it was discomforting that they did not see anyone waiting for them on the platform. They really began to feel apprehensive a few minutes later when a man approached them and quietly guided them out of the station. They were dead tired but had to walk for a few, long blocks without uttering a sound. The little girl was awake but had been fed so that she seemed quite comfortable, this time, in her father's arms. At the bend of one of the narrow streets, they noticed a covered truck parked under a dense tree. They were told to climb in and, to their delight, found some relatives waiting for them inside. They embraced and kissed fiercely and whispered a few words of heart-felt gratitude. The uncle who had come to fetch them hushed them up to keep quiet so as not to arouse any kind of suspicion. He had a business in town manufacturing ladders and owned a big truck that enabled him to deliver merchandise to different locations. A couple of heavy wooden ladders were placed on the sides of the truck and the uncle collapsed a third one into a convenient size that blocked the back entrance into the vehicle. He threw a large tarp on top of it that hid everything inside. It was very early in the morning; the train had pulled into the station around dawn and the streets were still quite deserted, and, thus, they were able and fortunate enough to reach their relatives' home without any incident.

The family was reunited and the newcomers, in time, became loyal, grateful citizens of their new country. The little girl, a grandmother by now, never forgot the tale of the boat ride that brought them to their final destination in Buenos Aires. Her eyes fill with tears each time she tells the story and, at times, when she sees firefighters carrying ladders or other people using them. After all it was her practical uncle who started a business with a product that everyone uses at one time or another; it made him prosper and symbolically helped his family climb out of the nightmares of World War II and into a better life.

Source Note

Based on an interview with Ana (Jane) Maria Karszenbaum in Buenos Aires, March 2002. Ana (Jane) is the cousin of Yeshayahu Birnbaum, a dear friend of the author, who lives in Israel.

Evita

On one of the walls of her elegant living room in Lima, Evita has an imposing picture of Machu Pichu painted by the eighty-year-old artist A. Granier. Close to it is a large, framed poster of a dark haired Spanish girl who is performing the flamenco, her graceful arms lifted high above her head, her hands holding castanetas that accompany her vivacious dance. The name Evita appears on the bottom of the poster, a humorous gift given to her by one of her relatives. It does not resemble her, which is quite obvious, since Evita is blond, her eyes are the color of the morning sky, and she is not young anymore, but it is Evita, nevertheless, in spirit. "I love life," she says, smiling, and her voice sparkles just as her eyes do. "I love people," she emphasizes, spreading her arms in a gesture of sincere affection, as if she is standing on top of Machu Pichu and ready to embrace the whole world.

Her parents were Jewish immigrants who escaped from Bolshevik Russia to Brazil, where they spent some years and where Evita and her brother were born. Life was hard and the climate did not agree with them either and so, in time, her family moved to Peru, to the small coastal town of Trujillo where her younger sister was born. Her parents were lovebirds from the very first time they met. Theirs is a story Evita likes to tell, the fair, blue-eyed, seventeen-year-old Mania, innocent and sweet, and the dark-eyed, handsome, fiery nineteen-year-old Herschel who won the girl's heart by dancing the *kazachok*. Evita is drawn to this precious memory, particularly since she also has many unhappy tales to tell and, by nature, gravitates towards the sunny and cheerful events in her life.

Evita also recalls another incident in her parents' life that shows how very naive and inexperienced they were and how vulnerable as well. When her parents arrived from Russia, from their little shtetl, they were so poor they did not even have a coat. They had a few coins and when they got off the boat, the one thing they wanted was food.

They walked into the very first eatery they saw. It was a cold night and they were glad to get into the warm restaurant and find a seat in a corner, where they enjoyed a bowl of hot soup. On their way out they noticed that, at the entrance, there was a coat rack with many garments hanging on it and, having been told about the marvels of the New World, assumed that they were put there for anybody's use. They carefully chose a couple of garments from the rack and profusely thanked the host in Russian and Yiddish. He answered with a smile and a torrent of words, none of which they understood. He watched them as they were crossing the street, quite obviously enchanted by Mania's beauty and youth. Later in life, when they understood that they had committed a bad deed, albeit unknowingly and unwillingly, they tried to make up for it by doing many *mitzvot* and helping the poor in their community in Trujillo, particularly by donating garments.

Trujillo was founded in 1534 by Peru's conquistador, Francisco Pizarro, who named it after his birthplace in Spain. It is about 560 kilometers north of Lima, its weather is mild all year long, and many families of nobles settled there in the old days, mainly to exploit gold and silver mines and the large sugar plantations. Although Spain gave Peru its language, religion, and rulers, the civilization of the Inca has left its traces throughout Peruvian culture. Archaeological excavations have uncovered impressive native remains. To the north are the ruins of the largest mud-brick city in the world, built by the Chimu, who ruled the coast before the Inca conquest. To the south of Trujillo lie the imposing Moche pyramids of the Sun and the Moon, which was the center of Moche power from 100 to 600 AD. To the west is Huanchaco, an Indian fishing village where fishermen still ride the waves in fragile reed boats called "caballito de totora," just as their predecessors did hundreds of years ago.[1] The "little horses of reed"— literally—are unusual, small boats that the fishermen ride, sitting on them like cowboys on horses. Using them as surfboards and relying on the waves to bring them ashore, they leave the boats on the beach once their day's work is done. These reed boats get so heavy with water that they need to be dried for quite a long period of time after being paddled and pulled up the shore.

Roman Catholicism has been the established religion of the country since 1915 but other religions are permitted and tolerated, and when Evita and her family moved to Trujillo, they found a tiny Jewish community that had clung together since the beginning of the twentieth century. There were about fourteen families who took care of each other. Whenever there was a celebration, a Bar Mitzvah, or any other kind of festivity, no invitations were needed; everyone was presumed invited and everyone went; they were all part of a family. Her parents were religious, particularly her mother; her father changed somewhat with the times. Evita has a lot of affection for Trujillo and the Indian community. She knows a little of the Quechua and Aymara native languages that are spoken in that area. She praises the kindness and sensitivity of the local population she learned to know since her childhood and is proud of their beautiful artistry, their pottery, jewelry, and woven products.

Evita's father had to become a peddler to support his family. He was young, strong, and adventurous, and the first Jew to establish the peddler's route to Santiago de Chuco in the Peruvian Sierra and to the town of Abancay. He traveled on a mule, and that was the part he enjoyed, since he went through magnificent landscapes and was an admirer and lover of nature. The valleys were full of forests, unique natural lakes, and snow-clad peaks. Abancay, itself, as the name in Quechua indicates ("The Valley of the White Lilies"), was quite a sight to behold. Evita's father went in search of gold for which the region was famous. It was, nevertheless, a dangerous task since there were always bandits waiting for prey in the mountains he had to cross in order to get to the town of Abancay. The roads between high peaks and deep cliffs were winding and, many times, in fact the greater part of the year, the weather was rainy and with low temperatures.

Once, on the way back home with the merchandise he had bought, he was very tired and decided to rest for a while on the side of the road. He built a fire around some stones and placed a few potatoes in the center. He had learned this from the natives in the Sierra and always enjoyed their dishes. He decided to take a nap while the *huatia*, the ancient name of the dish, was cooking. He took a few sips of the excellent anise drink for which Abancay is famous still today and fell asleep. When he woke up he realized that all he had—including the cooked potatoes—had been stolen and taken away from him. He felt lost and depressed but, nevertheless, thankful to God for saving his life since peddlers had often been killed while traversing those mountains.

While in Trujillo, Evita's father mastered chemistry and learned how to melt gold and create different kinds of coins. He became so knowledgeable that people came from afar to seek his advice on matters of chemistry. He also had a very beautiful voice that was appreciated, in particular, by the congregation, since he served as a cantor during the holidays. His rendition of the Kol Nidre was exceptionally breathtaking. Evita inherited the voice and musical talent from her father. Since there were no Jewish schools in Trujillo at that time, her father, who was very much aware of the importance of education, decided to send his children to Christian schools. Evita attended a convent where she was treated very kindly. The Mother Superior, Maria Magdalena, never tried to influence Evita into changing her religion. Her father had requested that from the nun and she never broke her promise. People in that little town, in those days, were kind and considerate and respected each other's beliefs.

Young Evita was very open-minded and free as a bird. She had many friends and fell in love with a young man who was not Jewish. They could not resist each other and married at an early age despite the objections they faced from both sides. Evita bore in her mind and heart the young romantic love her parents had experienced and sustained over the years and, maybe, felt and thought that hers would be the same. Unfortunately, her romance did not last long; the young couple did not have too much in common and realized that they had made a mistake. Shortly after her second daughter was born, they got divorced.

Evita believes that God is always looking down from above. Bearing that in mind, she did not become despondent and never gave up. She moved to Lima with her two little children, where she attended the university and studied cosmetology. When her father passed away, she helped her mother, who also had come to Lima, and opened a

Jewish restaurant in the city.

It was in Lima that she found meaning to her life as well as true happiness and fulfillment. Her mother was an excellent cook, the restaurant became famous, and people came from afar to enjoy the food. One day a middle-aged man walked in and ordered dinner. He was a well-to-do merchant from the United States who had come to Peru on business. It was in her mother's restaurant that he saw Evita for the first time. Evita was helping her mother that day and noticed that the man followed her with his eyes wherever she went. He came back many times, and each time she was impressed by his good manners and his knowledge of Yiddish. He was a Lithuanian Jew who had lived in Cuba and Guatemala before settling down in the United States. He was very appreciative of the food they served and Evita found him very quiet but interesting. One day, he stayed in the shop until closing time; Evita had to leave to take care of her children but he still kept sitting. After everybody had left, he approached Evita's mother and asked for a cup of coffee. When she served it to him, he told her, "I asked for a cup of coffee but, actually, I want to know whether you would like to be my mother-in-law." The rest is, as they say, history. Evita married him and, although he was much older, they were like two peas in a pod. Their marriage lasted for twenty-five years and was the happiest period of her life. Despite the early demise of her brother and other tragic events she has experienced, her best memories are those of her youth in the town of Trujillo and her second marriage with—as she puts it—the most wonderful man in the world. Her deep belief in God and the realization that in life one always gets compensation for one's suffering has brought blessings to her and her family.

Source Note
Based on the interview with Eva Silverman Aleman in Lima, Peru, August 2001.

Text Note
1. In Lake Titicaca, high up in the Peruvian Andes, totora reeds grow in the lake in bunches and form large floating surfaces on which the inhabitants of that region build homes, schools, and even rear sheep. The floating "Islands"

are quite stable but a person standing in one place for a long time can get his/her shoes wet. When there is a lot of rain and the level of water in the lake rises considerably, the wind might push these small surfaces and they will float and drift into Bolivian waters (both countries share the lake); "Meeting in Taquile," Yolanda Sala, *http://www.yolisala.8m.com/taquile.html*).

Sea Monsters

$\mathcal{M}$alvina grew up in Warsaw in the early years of the twentieth century. Her family had lived in the Polish city for generations and, although not orthodox, they followed the religious traditions carefully. Thus, she did not get any formal education, since it was not compulsory for girls to do so, but she was encouraged to study. The popular Yiddish book, *Tzenah Urenah*, was kept in almost every household. It was Malvina's favorite because it contained many wondrous tales from the Old Testament, commentaries, and ethical teachings. Warsaw was famous for its Jewish life a long time before the events of its ghetto uprising. For centuries the Jews of Warsaw were an inseparable part of the city's life and merged well into the urban fabric. They had a decent relationship with the Polish gentiles, spoke the language, enhanced the commerce, and sometimes even participated in politics. Nevertheless, they created a world of their own and had a very strong sense of identity that kept them apart from the rest of the Polish people. This helped fight assimilation but, on the other hand, also created alienation and separation from the Poles. Years later, when Malvina had already lived in Buenos Aires for a long time, she could never forget Warsaw, the way it used to be, and neither did all the other Polish Jews there who felt the same attachment and had many memories of the old country.

In 1929, Malvina set out on a voyage to Argentina to join an older married sister who had encouraged her to come and start a new life in America. She traveled by train to the French port of Cherbone and from there sailed with a large number of immigrants, from different European countries, to Buenos Aires. The ship was large but very crowded and she felt quite uncomfortable in its belly, where she was assigned a bunk bed, next to a family of seven. These were Jews from a little shtetl and, although they were friendly, she did not like to be there since the children were noisy and unruly. Thus, she preferred to spend as much time as possible on the upper decks and watch the sea and the ship's crew doing their work. She was able to enjoy the fresh air and the ocean breezes for a few days until the weather turned foul and she was confined for a while to the bottom of the ship. Her neighbors were all sick and she could not tolerate the smell of the children's vomit that, despite being cleaned up, lingered for hours. She tried to read the Bible as much as she could in order to keep her mind away from the unpleasant surroundings.

Malvina came across the story of Jonah and the whale and read it a few times. In a way, she felt like him, all bundled up in the huge fish's intestines, not knowing whether he will get out; but then—she thought—the end was a happy one, thanks to God's will. The whale did not seem to be such a horrendous creature after all. It was only later, when she overheard some sailors discussing monsters in the high seas and describing them that a sense of fear and doom crept slowly into her heart. She tried to tell herself that those were just legends but her mind could not fight her feelings of apprehension. The sound of the storm, its huge waves pushing the ship up and down, the noisy winds continually whistling and shrieking, the inescapable stench and ever-lasting moaning of the sick, and the cries of frightened children became a scary, obsessive, nautical trauma for her that lasted throughout the trip and lingered in her subconscious all her life.

Two days later, when the storm had subsided somewhat, feeling weak and feverish she made her way to an upper deck and held on tightly to the railing. The winds had calmed down a little but the motion of the ship was still pretty erratic and she started feeling nauseous. AND THEN SHE SAW IT—not too far from the bouncing ship, something that looked like a huge snake with a large head, shaggy mane, and many arms. The size and movement of the creature were difficult to judge but she thought it could easily reach the ship, wrap its arms around it, and crush it. She felt faint and, when she recovered somewhat and looked out again, saw a monstrous, roundish beast that had big, blue bulging eyes and hundreds of flaps around its body that seemed to bring it closer and closer to the vessel. . . . She was sure the monster was carnivorous and, not willing to wait any longer, ran to the first sailor she noticed on the deck and pointed to what she had seen. He fixed his gaze on the spot for a moment and his face relaxed into a good-natured grin. At first he told her that he was going to capture the monster and tow it all the way to Buenos Aires but, as he looked into the eyes of the frantic young woman, he realized she was not going to be amused by his jokes and tried to calm her down. He insisted that many times long pieces of seaweed can be taken for a serpent or octopus and that some giant squids can be found here and there in the oceans but that they are not dangerous. He tried to convince her that she was just imagining things based on some mysterious stories she had heard about creatures that do not exist. When he failed to convince her, he decided to go along with her request and promised to alter the course of the ship to escape the monster. He helped her downstairs to reach her bunk bed, where her compassionate neighbor, thinking that she was seasick, helped her to lie down.

Yet Malvina was sure of what she had seen and convinced that the creatures lived in the depths of the ocean and were after her and the other passengers on the ship. She was hoping that the sailor would keep his promise to choose a different course to reach America but had doubts as to whether he would or could do it. She thought of Jonah and the whale, and felt a real affinity with the hero of the Biblical story. That evening, while dining, she carefully concealed a knife in the folds of her dress, and put it under her pillow when she went to bed. It made her feel somewhat safer; she kept it there till the end the voyage when she returned it to the kitchen.

The weather improved and the sea calmed down. It was a beautiful sunny day when they reached the shores of Argentina, and she was happy to be greeted by her sister and brother-in-law who were waiting for her at the port. Looking at the blue, placid surface of the ocean, she should have known that the monsters had been figments of her imagination created by the difficulties of her voyage, yet in her heart she believed they did exist. Somewhere far down, in the remote depths of the seas, those mythical creatures were not extinct but in search of victims and she had been fortunate enough to escape that ordeal.

Malvina met her husband shortly after arriving in the New World.

He was also an immigrant from Warsaw and they had a lot in common. He, too, had arrived at the request of an older sister and worked with his brother-in-law in a textile factory. They had a very good reputation and succeeded in their business. Life was difficult and they kept the Jewish customs as much as they could. It was essential for them to work on certain Saturdays, so they could not always keep the Shabbat, but they ate kosher foods and kept the tradition of the holidays. On those occasions many members of the family celebrated and enjoyed each other's company as well as their reminiscences from the old country. Malvina and her husband had three sons who grew up in a very loving environment, one that was poor but full of music. No matter where they were, the parents loved to sing, not just in the synagogue but while they were working and at home. It was their family tradition to accompany daily tasks with songs and, thus, enrich their lives. In a way it merged beautifully with the Argentinean habit or tradition. The Argentineans were always very attached to folk music that has its roots in Spain, as well as in the rhythms of native people and immigrants from Africa. The Europeans, mainly Poles, Russians, and Germans, brought to the coastal areas of the country many popular melodies such as waltzes and polkas that had some influence on the local music as well.

The Polish Jews, in that epoch, never got over their longing for the old country, particularly Warsaw. They were not interested in becoming Argentinean citizens until after the end of the Second World War since they believed they would go back one day. They were aware of the atrocities that were taking place in Europe but would not admit it. They did not integrate with the gentiles, spoke Yiddish, and did not learn Spanish properly. A good Jewish education was considered essential and emphasized greatly. There were very popular Yiddish theatres in Buenos Aires in those times. Actors came to perform from abroad and Jewish cultural life was very rich. At one point in time, toward the end of World War II, a certain song became very popular; it was named "Warsaw" and its refrain, "Warsaw, you will once again become the great Jewish town you were," was sung continually by young and old alike, although they knew that the Warsaw of old did not exist anymore. They could not forget the places they had lived in—the homes, temples, and shops; the way they had been in the past. In their minds they would never become irretrievable; they could always summon the pictures and feel consoled, at least for a while. It was, of course, a case of complete denial; they needed the fantasy to survive, although they knew without any doubt that they were better off than their brethren in the Old World.[1]

Malvina was a very bright woman and could foresee the future. She wanted her children to get the proper secular education that would guarantee their success in life without leaving behind their Jewish roots. There was simply no ambiguity about that. The only things she was not sure about were the sea monsters she continued to believe in, and which kept her on her toes each time she came close to the sea and whenever she thought about them.

Source Note

Based on an interview with Professor Avraham Huberman in Buenos Aires, March 2002. The tale describes his mother's fear of the unknown as she sailed towards life in the New World.

Text Note

1. In July 1944, Isaac Bashevis Singer, who in later years was awarded the Nobel Prize in Literature, wrote in the New York Yiddish newspaper *Forverts*, "I know that the Jews have disappeared from Warsaw, but I cannot truly imagine it. When I say: 'Warsaw,' in my soul's eye I see the old, Jewish Warsaw. I see Jewish streets, vendors' stalls, synagogues, houses of study, marketplaces, courtyards full of Jewish inhabitants. Despite what I know, I cannot present Warsaw judenrien nor Jewish streets as heaps of rubble" (*http://jewish.sites.warszawa.um.gov.pl/wstep_a.htm*).

The Survivor

He came to Rosario when he was already in his early thirties with a wife and a young daughter. He was a Polish Jew with a zest for life and a will to survive looking for a new homeland in which to bring up his family. He had barely any education—except for what he had learned in the heder—since Jews in Poland in the days before World War II were not allowed to study. Thus he became a traveling salesman in a strange country trying to make a decent living in order to support his family. He liked the name Diamond that he had inherited from his ancestors and decided to continue the family tradition of selling jewelry, with a hope for a fresh start and good luck in his endeavor. There was not much he could invest in the venture and so he put together, in his small suitcase, an interesting and diverse collection of cheap trinkets, which were, nevertheless, of good quality. He had necklaces made of glass and beads, some shiny pins, earrings, bracelets, anklets, and a few opaque amulets and rosaries that were popular at that time with the natives of the town. He had also carefully put aside, in the inner pocket of his coat, a few semi-precious sparklers, medallions made of agate, jaspers, and quartz crystals, which were found in some regions of Argentina and considered valuable. And just to be on the safe side, in case he could not sell much of his wares initially, he also wore the gold watch that had belonged to his grandfather and which he would sell, albeit unwillingly, if absolutely necessary. The fancy watch also gave him a certain aura—an impression that he was a successful merchant, not just a vagrant vendor—that won the respect of his customers. Whenever he thought it was appropriate, he pulled out of his pocket the thick chain to which the heavy watch was attached and consulted the timepiece, implying that although very interested in the sale of a particular item he was also a very busy man.

Rosario was still a small town when the peddler and his family arrived. It was, however, far from being the tiny village it had been in the eighteenth century when people began to settle down along the river Parana, in an area also called Pago de Arroyos—Region of the Streams. It had grown around a chapel that had been dedicated to the Virgin of the Rosary, from which it got its name. The vast pastures had attracted many horsemen who prospered as local gauchos working their cattle. Rosario had welcomed people from all corners of the world; the peddler and his family were surrounded by foreigners of many nationalities who had come—just like them—looking for their fortune along the shores of the Parana River. They lived, like many others, in a small apartment, under bad conditions, and were easy prey for many diseases such as cholera, tuberculosis, and even bubonic plague. Yet circumstances improved and, in time, Rosario—thanks mainly to its flourishing port—became the second largest city in Argentina.

Diamond, the peddler, was very adaptable and had many ingenious ideas on how to market his merchandise despite one big obstacle, which was that he had no knowledge whatsoever of Spanish. He knew it would take him quite some time to learn what to him sounded like a very difficult tongue. He enjoyed the sound of it, which was melodious and pleasant to his ears, so different from the Polish and Yiddish he had heard all his life, but was concerned that his handicap would prevent him from selling the jewelry successfully. His merchandise was presented beautifully, hanging from little hooks he had attached to the inner lining of his suitcase, and, once sold, he also inserted the jewelry into colorful small pouches that his wife had sewn. He even had candies for the children of his customers who did, no doubt, appreciate his thoughtfulness.

Being so very uncomfortable with his lack of knowledge of Spanish, he decided to pretend he was a deaf-mute and thus, using sign language or writing down the price of the jewelry on pieces of paper, he hoped to do well. He did not have a bad conscience about his deception since he figured that he should not talk at all rather than use broken sentences and wrong words, which most probably would give a very bad impression. The main thing, he comforted himself, was to be honest and sell good merchandise for a reasonable price. To reach his customers he had a few methods; mostly he knocked on doors or clapped his hands, notifying them of his presence just the way many Jewish peddlers announced their business all over Latin America in those days.

He became extremely successful. He had a very pleasing personality and, being very jovial and good looking, used his broad smile to his advantage. People were compassionate and felt sorry for the poor deaf-mute peddler and, thus, they almost always bought something from him. In time he was able to provide his customers with more expensive jewelry and some pricey watches that were mailed to him from Buenos Aires. Watches became a great source of income to him. Not too many people owned watches in those days and they were considered very important, useful, and classy. He had a collection of mechanical watches and stop-watches, as well as one or two marine chronometers much valued by the sailors who frequented the port. He also sold a few plain as well as elegant chains and straps to which the watches could be attached. Diamond became not only very knowledgeable about the type of watches and clocks he carried, but also about the history of precision time-keeping instruments. A friend from the big city had sent him an old Polish book that dealt with the history of watches and he had prepared, with the help of his wife who had a gift for languages and had mastered Spanish very easily, a small pamphlet that he presented to his delighted customers.

His obsession with the watches was a source of pleasure to him but, ironically, also led to his downfall. For a few years he had prospered as a jewelry vendor and kept the secret of his fake handicap from almost everybody. His wife and daughter were the only ones who knew the truth and would have never disclosed it. Yet, one day while he was taking a short break in a local plaza eating his lunch, he happened to look at his favorite watch and realized that it had stopped. He shook it and brought it close to his ear, wondering what had happened. When he realized that the mechanism was not working anymore he became frantic since it was not just his beloved watch but also his good luck talisman. Loudly, he uttered a few curses in dismay and anger, and did not realize that on a nearby bench two of his customers were relaxing, enjoying their siesta. They were completely and utterly shocked when they saw him listening to his watch and cursing loudly when he realized that it had stopped and was broken. He kept shaking it over and over, muttering words of despair and rage until he suddenly became aware that some people were looking at him from afar. It did not take long for the community to learn about his deception and, although he had not cheated anybody with the merchandise he sold, his reputation was ruined. The word was out that he could talk and hear, and always had. He lost all his customers because they felt that he had made fools out of them and would not forgive him for what they perceived to be despicable behavior. Having no choice, with his business ruined, and no other means of survival, he left Rosario with his family and settled down far from there, close to the Chilean border, in the town of Mendoza.

For a while things did not go too well in Mendoza. The peddler did not want to pursue the jewelry business anymore and, in order to make a living, tried a variety of things until he found out that he could fare quite well in real estate. He had bought a very simple, small house in town in which the family was not very comfortable in the hot, humid summer days, but it was close to a tree-lined plaza and they had a wonderful view of Aconcagua, one of the highest mountains in South America. Diamond used to sit for hours in front of the window looking at the mighty peak and listening to music. He was a music lover and had listened to it all his life, even during his "deaf-mute" period when the melodies that were heard coming from his apartment were, supposedly, his wife's and daughter's favorites. He was a worshipper of opera, Puccini's *Tosca* being his favorite. He had learned everything on his own and also, over time, mastered Spanish very well. Shortly, he was able to survive without too much trouble by buying dilapidated houses, fixing them up as nicely as he could, and reselling them for a good profit. The labor was backbreaking since he could not afford help and did most of the repairs on his own. He knew the town very well after a while, and his sales talent helped him to make a name for himself as a very competent and forceful but honest real estate agent. As time went by, he began suffering from extremely intense back pains that were a result of the many years of hard toil. The optimistic, life-loving man became an unhappy, moody, and suffering individual who did not seek to communicate with others and, in time, became a recluse. His lust for life dissipated, and he found no joy in mere survival anymore. The end of his journey was a very sad one since he had lost all the zest and joy for life he had known in his younger years, and, not being able to cope with his physical pain and mental anguish, gave up his will to live.

Source Note

Based on an interview with Adriana Balter in Santiago, Chile, March 2002, in memory of her maternal grandfather whom she wants to remember as the strong, ingenious, life-loving man he had been most of his life.

The Mortician

"Call no man happy until you know the nature of his death ..."
—Herodotos, *History Book I*, Chapter on Solon, the Greek lawmaker

The light, blue color of his eyes and their transparency create the impression that a person could reach the depths of his soul without making too much effort, yet gazing into them attentively, there is mainly emptiness, as if most of what he has felt and experienced during his life has been washed away, over the years, by floods of suffering and misery. Nevertheless, he watches people cautiously, as if he is concerned there might be some danger lurking around the corner. He is a sad, old man who does not smile very often, and he lives in a small apartment on the third floor of a residence for elderly people in Quito, the capital of Ecuador. The place is very modest but neat and clean. On the walls he has photos of his departed wife and his only son, who is living in the United States. This is a world he feels safe and comfortable in, an enclave away from all that has happened in the past, particularly in those distant days in Europe. He talks slowly yet willingly, dwelling on the harsh details of his past, savoring them, as if telling about them lightens his burden, giving him hope that his tale will not be forgotten. He is the manager of the Jewish cemetery in town, as well as the mortician. He holds an important position, one that brings him respect and acknowledgement from the community; he cherishes these as rewards he would not have been able to enjoy otherwise.

We have been talking in the corner of the dining room of a hotel in downtown Quito. His long, pale fingers move languidly along the pattern of the tablecloth, caressing it and feeling it, as if it were not an object but the body of a recently deceased. He is the one who would be giving it the last rites, cleansing it gently and respectfully before the burial. He would not see it as just a cadaver that would be decomposing in a short while but as a person who had lived his or her life and was going to be laid to rest with dignity, following the rituals of Judaism, the way it is supposed to be. He had sworn to it on the piles of dead, abused bodies he had seen so many times. He had promised the Almighty one day—while being drenched and cold, lifting his head to the dark, angry skies, there in far away Europe—that if he survived the inhumane ordeal of the war, he would always make sure that no dead body would be buried as a dog. He would, if it were within his power, take care of any Jew who died and bury him according to Jewish customs.[1]

Shrul Solon was born in the town of Chotin in Bessarabia in 1920.[2] In those days that region did not belong to Russia but to Romania. In 1918, when World War I was over, the great empires collapsed, the English and the French dominated Europe, and the Russians lost Galicia. Hungary and Czechoslovakia became autonomous, and Austria and Germany remained on their own. Life as a child was pleasant in Chotin, where he went to a heder and liked to visit the small synagogue his father frequented. There were places of worship on almost each street corner. The population of twenty-one thousand inhabitants included about ten thousand Jews who had a very good relationship with the Christians. The Jews lived mostly on the main street and the gentiles respected their habits and customs. On Fridays and holidays, the peasants and others did not come to sell their wares or shop after noon, aware of the Shabbat and the sacred Jewish days. Shrul Solon remembers vividly the Shabbat celebration and the ritual baths, the special clothes they wore, the way his father and grandfather dressed up in long black coats and hats, and slowly, using an elegant cane, made their way down the street to the temple. In the meantime, his mother prepared a delicious meal; he can still smell the fresh, golden *challah* she baked, the chicken soup with farfellos or rice, and the gefilte fish. His father sat at the head of the table, his mother to his right, the boys to the left of their father, and the girls next to their mother. The Shabbat candles were lit, the blessing over the wine was performed, and they each got a piece of the fragrant challah. At the end of the meal they sang some songs and then the children were allowed to go outside and play a little before bedtime.

Thus time passed; he went to the heder and also to a secular school to study Romanian and general subjects. Life was quite peaceful until about 1936 when anti-Semitism took over. Since 1930, the Iron Guard had become the country's most powerful party. These were fascists whose philosophy was very close to that of the Nazis. They blamed the Jews, communists, and liberals for Romanian economic problems, which had started with the worldwide depression in 1929. The Iron Guard used brute force against their opponents, and the Romanian King Carol, who was concerned about their influence, declared himself dictator and outlawed all political parties.

Life became very harsh for the Jews; many lost their jobs and sources of income, and they were considered second-class citizens. In the province of Bessarabia, their citizenship was actually taken away from them and, in order to keep their property, they had to prove that their families had resided in that part of Romania since before 1918. They were forced to open their shops on Saturdays, civil rights were denied to them, and policemen would stop them on the streets to order them not to speak Yiddish, insisting that Romanian be their only language of communication.

Things became even more difficult. At the start of World War II, Romania remained neutral for a while but the Germans kept expanding their power. They allowed Hungary to swallow Transylvania and a part of Romania. Russia got Bessarabia and a part of Bukovina. Bulgaria also helped herself to a section of Dobrudja, which used to be Romanian territory. The king lost his popularity due to these events and gave up the throne to his son, Michael, whose prime minister, Ion Antonescu, became the de-facto ruler. Antonescu sided with the Germans and, in late 1940, Romania joined the German side. Antonescu added Iron Guard members to his government, which was declared a Nationalist-Legionary State. A "legionary police" was organized based on the Nazi model and many anti-Semitic atrocities were committed.

In 1940, the Russians occupied that part of Romania where Chotin is located. There had been a lot of communist propaganda preceding these events, and young people were particularly vulnerable to the new ideas. Those who subscribed to the communist ideology had been in great danger; some of them were expelled from colleges, others killed, and many left the town. Solon stayed in Chotin. With the Russian occupation, some Jews gained important positions since they sympathized with Communism more than the Christians did. Those who objected to it were shot and, at times, corpses lined the streets.

When the war started, the Germans bombarded Chotin and destroyed the bridge connecting that part of Bessarabia, where the Russians had set up their camp, with the other side of the Dniester River that was already the Ukraine. The Russians promptly rebuilt a temporary one through which tanks and trucks could pass, but in the depth of the night or at dawn the Germans kept coming and destroying the bridge over and over again. The homes of the Jews were almost completely demolished since most of their dwellings were on the main road leading from Tchernovits to the bridge. In July of that year, the Romanians and their new German allies entered Chotin and started executing whoever they saw. For a whole week the Jews did not dare come out of their devastated homes and the peasants that came from the countryside looted whatever they could. When they finally had to get out, they were forced into labor, in particular on the cleanup of the roads. One Friday, an order was given that everybody had to take a rucksack, fill it with whatever each person could, and be ready to leave. They marched for days without end, and found that the Jews had been killed in almost all the little towns and villages they passed on their way. They did not know where they were going. In each place they were forced to do hard work; those who could not cope were killed at once. One night Solon was woken up, taken immediately to the road, with just his shirt on, and ordered to march. He walked with others who shared his fate, for four days and four nights, to a place where there was a need to repair a road that had been destroyed and was full of huge potholes created by heavy equipment, such as tanks, as well as the bombs that had fallen. The length of the damaged section was about twenty kilometers, and he worked there until the end of September, at which time he and the others were ordered to march back to a ghetto in Bessarabia. Their numbers kept dwindling; those who could not walk were killed and many had already died during the four months of hard labor. They crossed the Dniester in a leaking boat, were divided into small groups, and put to work on anything that was necessary. Solon stayed there for three years. The conditions in the camp were atrocious. There was only one water well that served hundreds of people. There were no restrooms available and people just did what they had to do wherever they could. When snow began thawing in the spring, water seeped into wells, carrying with it the human waste that was all around them. Diseases began affecting people and they started dying. His mother, who had been brave and very supportive despite all the agony and hardships they went through, got sick and died of dysentery, and that was just the way his father passed away a few months later. His only brother was also working nearby and Solon was able to see him, from a distance, once in a while, but after his mother passed away, the bond they all shared had broken. His mother had been a very intelligent woman, with the gift for saying the right thing at the appropriate time, and she kept them from giving in to despair. Once she was gone, the tie that held them together as a family withered away.

The nightmare of hard labor continued. Day after day he was assigned to roadwork and had to carry huge stones and rocks, then cut them in two, three, or four pieces to create metric squares that were used for repairs. On occasions when he did not succeed in completing the job, he was not given any food, which was very scarce anyway. They gave the prisoners three hundred grams of bread a day and twice a day a thin watery soup with a little bit of cooked rice. His work started at six in the morning and at times he had to walk, for almost a whole day or during the night, from one place to another location, wherever his labor was required.

One day, Solon and ten other men and women were ordered to deliver some tobacco to the Germans in a distant location. They were allowed to rest near a farm that evening. Solon was almost blind; he could not see anything at night and very little during the day, and his vision kept deteriorating constantly. He found an opportunity to hide and stayed behind. It was a desperate move, but he managed to mingle with other prisoners who worked in that place and lucked out. His absence went unnoticed. A cook who prepared food for the prisoners who worked there took a liking to him, particularly since Solon spoke Russian and Ukrainian and mainly because he was ready to do anything and everything for a little bit of food. Solon peeled potatoes and carried heavy buckets of water that left his arms sore and completely numb; he cut wood until his fingers bled but he was glad to do it all because at night he could crawl into the field without being noticed and eat carrots. . . .He had heard a doctor say once that carrots were good for the eyesight and so he spent a few hours every night eating the dirty carrots he pulled out of the soil without daring to wash them so he would not be caught. After a few weeks his eyesight did improve.

He stayed in that area until November of 1942. The bitter cold of the Ukrainian countryside drove some people to despair. Many froze to death since they had no blankets and were exposed to the harsh winter elements day and night. They slept by embracing each other—men, women, old or young, it really did not matter; they were exhausted, half-dead, and hungry; they just wanted to feel some warmth and the only source was the heat of the other miserable human bodies that shared their fate. An order came and Solon and his group had to cross a bridge leading to Odessa. They had no idea what was awaiting them. They found many people from all the regions of Romania and Bessarabia. Solon's desolation, grief, and desperation made him brave, and he helped a group of guerillas that was trying to sabotage the Germans. He aided, in particular, one young man whom he gave the Jewish identification card he had taken from a dead comrade and, thus, the fearless guerilla was able to pass into the zone that was guarded heavily by Germans, who allowed only prisoners to cross the bridge for their daily labor. Later Solon heard that the young fighter had not been successful after all; he had been caught and executed.

Solon was liberated in 1944 and returned to his native town, yet his troubles were far from over. He tried to find somebody alive but this search was hopeless; everyone he knew was dead. He went to the police quarters to get papers since he did not have any. His brother had been sent by the Russians to work in the Urals, to the town of Svetlosk, and for a while he lost touch with him.

Solon was drafted into the army and taken by train to a certain camp. Along the way, they came under heavy bombing and there were many casualties. He found himself buried under a pile of steel and earth, and felt more dead than alive. They told him that three days later the Russians came to check the wreckage and saw his head sticking out of the rubble. When one of the soldiers asked him if he was alive, he was able to nod a little despite the fact that he could not talk and could barely breathe. They loaded all the injured, the surviving victims, on a train and took them to Siberia, where he found himself in a hospital. When he recovered, he was in the army once again. Because he was injured they gave him lighter work for some time, and his name was changed from Srul to Sergei, since the Siberian girl who was filling out his papers did not understand what his name was. That is the name he has used since then. He thought his troubles were over but, once again back in Chotin, he came down with malaria and thought he was going to die. Nevertheless, he recovered once again and in August had to register at the Army headquarters, at which time he was told that he was to be sent to Japan. He was sure that that would be the end of him, but God is merciful; just before he had to leave, he learned that the Americans had dropped the Atom bomb on Hiroshima and the war was finally and truly over. When he found out that he had escaped another ordeal, he broke down for the first time since the War began and cried for a long time. He found some work and stayed there until March of 1946, when Stalin allowed a few Jews to leave, and he found himself once again back in Romania.

For a whole year he lived in unbelievable poverty. Jews, in general, could not find any work since they were considered traitors and had to survive by trading in the black market. He got in touch with a distant relative in Ecuador through the Jewish World Congress. Three months later, after a long and devastating hardship and terrible difficulties, he was able to obtain the proper papers for Ecuador. Hundreds of people wanted to get out, and the wait was extensive and desperate. In December of 1947, he flew from Bucharest to Prague. The airplane was full of people—more Jews than Christians—lawyers, doctors, rabbis, and *shochets*. They were jailed upon arrival since they had no transit visas. Solon had nothing, just a torn suitcase, a sweater, a shirt, and five detachable collars that he cherished because that was the old-fashioned way to wear a shirt. He had only one shirt, so at least he was able to change the collars and look more or less presentable. Some of the rabbis that were there called the American Jewish Joint Distribution Committee and a delegation came and got them out. Each person was taken to a different place. Solon was put up in a hotel, a plain one, but for him it was a palace. He had to walk a long distance to a restaurant that was affiliated with the Jewish Committee of New York and where he could get free meals. There were people from all over Europe, hungry, starved, and penniless. When a waiter brought some bread, everyone sitting around the table threw himself on top of it and before Solon realized it, all the bread was gone. Thus it happened many times. A man, who was watching Solon, came over and whispered in his ear that he would simply go hungry if he did not do what the others were doing. And, so, Solon learned to fight for the bread. The food was very scarce and was not enough. At night he was so starved that he went out and stole whatever food he could from the market stalls, whether it was an apple, a pear, or an onion—anything he could find. He stayed in Prague for about two weeks, after which he was able to leave for Paris by train. While at the station, he suddenly heard his name and a voice in Yiddish calling him. It was a countryman whom he had not seen for years. Solon told him he did not know where to go, and his friend took him to a hotel where other countrymen were living. It was a dirty, dilapidated place but it did not matter to them at all. There was just one bed—without a mattress—for two people, a small table, and a chair. When he got there, word went out that there was a countryman who had just arrived; everybody came out of their rooms and, whether he knew them or not, they hugged him, kissed him, and told him, "Zorg soch nisht," meaning "not to worry." Each person brought something— a chunk of challah, a piece of bread, a fruit—and it was of great comfort to him. After a few months he received some money from the Jewish authorities and finally was able to travel to Ecuador.

He reached Ecuador on July 17, 1948. A countryman was waiting for him in Quito, with whom he stayed for a while. The man helped him start a small business of peddling, and for four years he was barely able to make a living. During this period he met and married a woman who was also from his old country, all alone, and just as desolate as he was. She was a relative of the people who had helped him, to whom he was very grateful and whose friendship he treasured. Neither of them had anything, but they got married and managed with some basic help from friends. Those big-hearted people got a bed for them, some sheets, a stove for cooking, and brought them food for a week, as well as paid the small apartment's rent for three months. They were rich, in comparison, old timers in Ecuador who had arrived in 1938 with some money and owned a shop.

Solon's living conditions were very spartan for quite a while; his wife cooked simple food—mainly potatoes and rice—but he did not care; he was not hungry anymore, and it took him a long time to get used to the idea that he would have food the next day as well. As a peddler he sold merchandise for a few years and barely survived. There were five thousand Jews in Quito—Czechs, Germans, Hungarians, and Austrians. Many of them were intellectuals but not capable of making a living since they could not master the language. They lived on what the Jewish community gave them as well as the goods and property they had brought from their countries. Many died of illness, of desperation, and despair. Solon saved money, little by little, and was eventually able to open a small shop. His tiny fabric shop grew bigger and bigger and became a successful business, which he ran for twenty-five years. All that time he was interested only in survival, having a roof over his head, food to eat, and money to pay the rent for the shop. In time his wife was able to acquire fancier clothes and some jewelry, but Solon felt he did not need much for himself, hardly anything material during all those long years he toiled and succeeded. His son was born in 1952, almost four years after his marriage. It is his only son since his wife had a heart condition and was afraid to bear more children. Solon understood the importance of a good education and, despite the fact he could barely afford it, managed to send his son to an American school starting from kindergarten. Life was always a struggle;

most Jews were peddlers or small businessmen, and the competition was fierce, yet survival was not a nightmare anymore.

Solon had learned Spanish from a Russian-Spanish book he had purchased in Europe and knew a little when he arrived in Ecuador. He was one of the "verdes"—green ones—but there was already a small Jewish community in Quito when he got there and they gave him some support. The synagogue had been founded in the year 1928 and it grew in time, particularly when the Germans arrived; soon thereafter, they had a cantor from Germany, and later one from Poland. The local Indians respected the Jews and worked as servants to the gringos. His wife was able to have two maids after their son was born. Slowly, they got accustomed to the idea that there was no need to fear that something horrible would happen any time or that there would be no food to eat.

He kept his shop until the year 1978 when his wife died and his son left for Israel to study. He now lives by himself and is quite lonely. He emphasizes that he does not have many friends, since those exist only when one has money and carries on a business. It is enough for him that, being the mortician, a very important member of the Jewish Community in Quito, he is invited to every Bar Mitzvah, wedding, and celebration that takes place. And thus he lives in his small apartment and finds solace in the fact that life, at the end of his journey, is tranquil and there is no menace and danger to be faced upon awakening each morning. He is at peace.

His Spanish has never lost its East European accent; somehow it sounds appropriate, as if the Romanian intonation gives it more authenticity in describing the horrors of his experiences during the war. It is already dusk and our interview is at its end. Elegant, dim lamps light the restaurant and the tablecloth is by now dusted lightly with the ashes that fell through the skylight. The Tungurahua volcano has been active for two days and, although it is about two hundred kilometers from the capital, has polluted the air, and the dark ashes have been carried by the wind far from where it erupted, solemn messengers of the devastation it has created, as well as symbolic reminders of those who lost their lives in the ovens of the concentration camps. We say goodbye and, when I hug him, I see tears in his eyes, something he has been fighting those two hours we spent together. The taxi pulls away from the curb, he waves, and is gone—yet his story is with me to stay.

Source Notes

Based on an interview with Mr. Sergio Solon in Quito, Ecuador, August 2001.

Text Note

1. Solon's name goes back to ancient Greece, to the famous bearer of the same name, the lawmaker Solon (c. 638–559 B.C.). Sergio Solon knows that he has some Greek roots but that is all he was told; he has no idea from where the previous generations of the Jewish Solon family came before they settled down in Romania.

2. Some parallels to Sergio Solon's life story, especially his commitment to the Jewish burial rituals, may be found in "The Grateful Ghost," a Sephardic Jewish folktale from Turkey retold by Josepha Sherman in the Fall 2002 issue of *Parabola*.

Heritage films: The Eastern European Connection (*http//www.heritage-films.com/ROMANIA*).

A Dog's Loyalty

Many years ago, in the heart of Patagonia, way before the *estancias* came into being and most people lived on small farms, a family of Marranos that had fled from Spain settled down near the Negro River.[1] No one knows how they had arrived there and nobody asked, since the local population of Indians was not hostile, having themselves escaped the Spanish rule that had dominated the country since 1516. The people in that dry, desolate, and wind swept plateau of Southern Argentina survived mainly on raising sheep because the poor soil and lack of rain made it impossible to farm. Their modest dwellings were built close to the canyons that provided shelter from the harsh winds and violent storms.

The family owned a small hut with adobe walls that were whitewashed and the roof made of straw and mud. The dirt floor was disconcerting to the mother, who swept it many times during the day to keep the house neat and clean. She was an older woman who took good care of her son and nursed her ailing husband who, most of the time, was not able to tend to the sheep. A mestizo helped with the work in return for food.[2] He had appeared from nowhere one day and asked for some water to drink. Too skinny to cast a shadow, gaunt and weak, he could hardly stand on his feet. The mother, who was a kind-hearted soul, gave him some food and water. Since then, he had appeared every day and helped out without asking for any payment in return, just the food the mother made, which he devoured with zest. He told them that he had a hut near the canyon to which he retired every evening with a faithful dog that accompanied him everywhere.

It was obvious that the man was a gaucho and knew how to handle animals. He took care of the only horse the family had, as well as the sheep that, along with the son, he helped to tend. When asked where he had come from and where his family was, he told them his name was Juan and that he had no family of his own. He had come all the way from

Tierra del Fuego. As rugged as he was and unwilling to share any information about his former life, he was, nevertheless, a kind man, and the love that he bestowed on his dog was touching. The animal returned its master's devotion and never left his side. It was a female dog—large, shaggy, and dark—that had been with Juan since she had been a puppy.

One Saturday, as was their habit on a Shabbat, the family was not working but just resting by the entrance to their hut. The father was reading from a prayer book that was wrapped in an old newspaper. They had been used to concealing it since their days in Spain and, although they knew nobody was going to challenge their religion in their new land, they could not shake the fear and preferred to cover the old brown, decaying cover of the Hebrew book with the newspaper. Juan never came on Saturdays nor did he work on Sundays, for his own reasons.

As they were sitting quietly, enjoying a mild afternoon, a rider appeared on the horizon and soon enough they saw an officer of the law approaching their dwelling. He came from a village that was quite far from their farm, and they were surprised to see him dismount and approach their house. The man came to warn them that they were on the lookout for a criminal, a murderer who had escaped and not been found. They were searching everywhere for the dangerous, evasive man and were ready to pay a price for any good lead. The mother and father exchanged looks and the son grew pale, but none of them said anything about the man with the dog who helped them. The policeman left, warning them to be cautious since the criminal could be hiding anywhere and cause them harm.

When the horse and the rider disappeared over the other side of the canyon, the father and mother discussed the situation in hushed whispers. The son shared their opinion that Juan could not be a murderer. They had known him only for a few months but he just did not seem to have the makings of a criminal. They felt that it was a mistake even to think of him that way and decided to warn him about the policeman's visit, especially since he was so secretive and mysterious and might have something else to hide after all. Juan denied any such hideous deed as a murder and they believed him. The whole incident was soon forgotten.

A few weeks later, while Juan was outside his own dilapidated shack, he suddenly saw in the distance two officers on horses riding in his direction. He knew that there was no way he could explain anything to them since he was a mestizo; they would not trust him and would consider him a criminal, whether he was a murderer or not. He panicked and ran straight to the river, yet just as he reached its banks, the policemen fired their guns and he fell into the water mortally wounded.

Juan's dog had been inside the hut and came out running and barking as soon as she heard the commotion. She saw the men dismounting near the hut and ran straight back into the dwelling. The policemen had a good laugh; they mocked the dog and even lowered their rifles, so sure were they that the cowardly animal would not dare to fight them. Yet, in the twinkle of an eyelid, they saw the dog running out of the hut holding something in her mouth. One of the officers threw a couple of stones after the dog, cursing the animal for its cowardice. Yet the bitch ran straight to the bank of the river where her master was lying halfway in the water. She kept pulling at his sleeve until the dying man opened his eyes and looked for a moment at the dog and the rifle she was carrying. The eyes of the bitch were moist as if she was crying, and the sadness and concern Juan saw there were too much for him to bear. The officers by then had seen the rifle and were afraid to approach. Juan took the rifle from the dog and for a moment it seemed as if he was going to get up but he was not able to. All he could do was to pull away with great effort from the desperate bitch. Then, calling her by her name, he looked at her lovingly and fired a single shot straight into her head. When the police approached the scene they found both the master and his dog already dead.

Source Note

Based on IFA (Israeli Folktale Archives) # 8154, an Argentinean tale told from memory by Gyorah ben Mashi and recorded by Yifrach Habib.

Text Notes

1. Estancias – Huge ranches in the Pampas of Patagonia as well as other places during the 1800s.

2. Mestizo – A person of mixed origin—Indian and European.

Clara and the Gypsies

$\mathcal{D}$orka, a Romani gypsy, was on her way home from the festival. It was summer time, late afternoon, and she felt very tired. She had left her stall guarded by her brother, who was much better at selling her wares than she had ever been. She had sold some of her handmade necklaces, puppets, and dolls, and those that were left would be given away at half price if at all. Her brother would also make their small bear play the fiddle and collect some coins. The buzz and the noise of the streets left her with a severe headache, and she was anxious to reach the quiet, somewhat hilly area of the town with its deeply rutted paths, which were quite impassable even in horse drawn carriages. She looked back at the beach where the fair was taking place. She liked the beautiful town of Varna, located on the shores of the Black Sea, and loved to watch the setting of the sun over the horizon. Moonlight made the scenery even more magical but she hardly ever had time for that since in the evening she was busy cooking for and feeding her two children and her husband, although many times he was drunk and asleep when she reached home. Gyorgy had found refuge in liquor since the time he had been beaten up savagely by a group of Bulgarian youths who called him a tramp and hated him just for being a gypsy. They had been scapegoats for many ills in many countries, and no matter where they went they were blamed for one thing or the other. Dorka sighed and gathered the ample skirts of the colorful yet gaudy dress she wore to the fair. She tied the lower skirt to the outer one in order to be able to walk with greater ease on the bumpy, dusty path and not soil the garment that she would have to wear again the next day.

Suddenly she heard a moan and a cry coming from an area on one side of the road. She stopped walking and listened carefully. It had sounded like the voice of a small child or an animal in pain. Night was falling and the gray shadows of twilight were creeping all over the place. She could not see very well anymore. Once again she heard the heartbreaking noise and following it, rather then looking for a particular spot, she saw the outline of what seemed to be a ditch or a big hole. She kneeled to look inside and saw a small girl, curled up in the bottom of the pit, moaning and weeping. She called out to her to hold on and went running to her home, which was nearby, to get help. Luckily her husband was quite sober that evening and followed her back to the place carrying a small ladder. They pulled the child out of the hole, wrapped her in a blanket, since the night was getting cold, and took her to their home and placed her on a bed. The little girl, about six years old, was quite terrified at first but, when they gave her some milk to drink and Dorka gently applied a cold, wet towel on the leg which had been injured, she calmed down and told them that her name was Clara and that her family lived nearby, in the Jewish ghetto. She had been walking around and playing all by herself and had not noticed the pit until it was too late and she had already fallen into it, hurting her ankle.

Dorka watched the little girl as she fell asleep and realized that she had to notify the family so as to avoid being accused of child kidnapping. No matter how good her intentions, she would be blamed for an evil deed unless she found the parents and explained to them what had happened. Quickly she put some food on the table and, covering herself with a shawl, left for the Jewish section that was not far from where they were encamped. That part of town was also run-down, although it was in better shape than the gypsy's camp. Fortunately, the moon was shining brightly that night and Dorka did not have much trouble in reaching the first houses. She saw some dim lights flickering from the narrow windows. It was Friday evening and the Jews had lit their Shabbat candles. She knocked on the first door and an elderly woman opened it partially, eyeing her with suspicion. Dorka explained her situation and asked whether they knew where Clara's family lived. An old man came out and led her to one of the even smaller huts at the end of the dusty, winding road. She thanked him and knocked on the gate. A woman opened the door and Dorka could see about a dozen children sitting around the table with a man at the head of it. He was praying and the woman, whose eyes were red and whose face was swollen as if she had been crying for a long time, looked at Dorka with surprise and some fear. When Dorka told the woman that she had found her little girl, she grabbed her by the shoulders, embraced her tightly, and pulled her into the house. With great excitement she told her family the news, using a strange sounding yet very melodic language. All jumped up, surrounded Dorka, and began hugging her gratefully. It seems they had been looking for Clara all evening but could not find her and, when night fell, began praying for her, awaiting daylight to continue their search.

Dorka told them that Clara was safe and sound asleep, and suggested they take the little girl to a doctor in the morning since her injury seemed to be quite serious—her ankle was swollen and there was a deep cut all the way to the knee. Clara had apparently fallen on some broken bottles that had been thrown into the pit and lost a lot of blood. Her family was very poor and did not have the money to pay a doctor. Thus the kind-hearted Dorka offered to take care of Clara using some herbal ointments that the Romani are very good at, medicines that they had used for many generations and which were, most of the time, beneficial. Clara's mother was unable to give her the expert care Dorka could provide and, in a way, felt grateful as well as relieved since she had eleven children at home to take care of, four of them younger than Clara. Clara also seemed to like it in the gypsies' home—it was a converted old bus—and since they were so anxious to help, the girl's family decided to leave her with the Romani's until she recovered. Thus a great friendship began, blossomed, and was there to stay until the day the Jewish family had to leave Varna in search of a better life.

Dorka became a second mother to Clara. When the little girl recovered and was able to walk again despite her limp, she sometimes had trouble deciding where to sleep and with which family to spend her day. She considered Dorka's two children her siblings as well, and Dorka's husband a good-natured, mild-tempered uncle whose tales she would remember all her life. When not drunk and sleepy, Gyorgy liked to help around the house and tell stories. He never ventured too far from his home, and his wife, children, as well as other members of the gypsy clan, took care of him since he was, at times, somewhat confused.

Clara knew something about the history of her own people, who had arrived in Bulgaria from Salonika. A few of her relatives had lived in Macedonia in the distant past after having fled from the Spanish Inquisition and had established themselves as merchants in their new country. Some of them were luckier than others and became successful. Clara's family was not one of them. Her parents had to struggle hard to make a living and make ends meet. Just like the gypsies', the Jews' fate was a seesaw in the hands of different governments over the years. Nevertheless, they did fare better than the Romani tribes since some of the members of the Jewish community were wealthy, influential, and respected by the rulers. These periods did not last very long as the principle of equality did not really exist for the minority groups, and they were discriminated against in one form or another. By the time Clara, as a young woman, left Bulgaria in the early 1930s because of the fear of an imminent war, there remained only a handful of Jews in Varna. She was traveling to Chile to marry the man her family had found for her, thanks to a distant relative, and her heart was full of anticipation and hope. She had grown up during very difficult times, had known lots of hardships, but hers was a sunny disposition. Her love of life, her musical and artistic inclinations, which she had inherited from her second family rather than the one she was born into, were a guiding light all her life.

Gyorgy had told her about the origins of the Romani people, how they had come, just like the Sephardic Jews, from faraway lands in search of success and happiness. When lucid, he could talk for hours, pause at times for a while as if he was daydreaming, and then burst into a sweet sounding song expressing sadness at the destiny of his own people. He had a poetic soul and a big heart and there was not one evil bone in his body. Even when drunk, which seemed to be his only weakness, he was gentle and considerate, and never condemned those who had caused him to become what he was. The Romani Chovinaho—shaman—had given up on healing him and only came to visit him once in a while to see how he was doing.

Because of his mental condition, Gyorgy was also considered a fortuneteller, although in Gypsy society only women traditionally dealt with that, yet Gyorgy was really one of a kind. Clara had heard many folk-tales that the gypsies retold during long evenings sitting at a fire—stories about witches, goblins, and fairies that had originated in India and been transplanted into many countries over the centuries. The gypsies considered these stories to be real and believed that they carried profound messages. Clara never forgot those magical evenings around the fire. She participated in their dancing, which she loved and was very good at despite her slight limp since the damaged leg had never healed completely. Nevertheless, when at home, she was able to detach herself from the Romani's way of life and follow the simple rules of Judaism that her family embraced. They were not religious but tradition was of great importance to them, and Clara always kept that in her heart. Despite the Romani saying, "With one behind you cannot sit on two horses," she seemed to be able to live with both families without losing the attachment to either one of them. One of her greatest friends was Badu, the bear. He was a very old animal that had been caught in the forests of Russia a long time ago and sold to Dorka and her clan. They taught him a few tricks, which he performed nicely, and was taken good care of as a reward. He had learned to play the violin; he could hold it under his chin with one paw and move the bow over the strings. He did not know any melodies and was somewhat deaf. The notes he produced were off-tune, scratchy, and annoying, yet the sight of him holding the old fiddle and playing with his eyes closed made people stand still, watch him silently, and drop a few coins each time he finished a gig. He was a very sad looking bear indeed.

Dorka had given Clara a gift when she left her home after the injury had healed sufficiently. It was a lovely colorful necklace made of different kinds of beads, at the end of which was a small pouch made of some shiny fabric. "Carry it inside your blouse, dear girl," Dorka had told Clara. "The pouch seems to be empty but it is not like that all the time. Every night before you go to sleep, you will untie the strings and empty all the invisible troubles and concerns that have accumulated during the day and thus, the next morning, you will have a fresh start and hopes for a happy day."

Clara lived in Chile for many years and had a very rewarding life;

people were drawn to her mirthful spirit and loved her dearly. The Sephardic community in Santiago still remembers her zest for life, the festivities she helped to arrange for them, and the foods she prepared, particularly the delicious pies and eggplant and lamb dishes she was so well known for. Most of all, they remember what a wonderful dancer she had been. Small, somewhat stocky, and rounder as time went by, she was still very agile and performed beautifully, singing and dancing to her heart's content at any festive occasion. Anybody who watched her would be pulled into the circle she created and joyfully dance with her in celebration of life and hopes for good things to come. She always remembered the gypsies with great affection, cherished the necklace that Dorka had given her, and never failed to empty the contents of the pouch until her very last day on earth.

Source Note

Based on an interview with Camila Benado, granddaughter of Clara Calderon Cohen, in Santiago, Chile, March 2002. Benado is a journalist who works at the Ministry of Labor in Santiago.

Ode to a Dead Son

$\mathcal{H}$e reached the shores of Argentina by mistake. The year was 1891 and as a young Jew from the Ukraine, unable to study medicine in his homeland, he hoped to fulfill his dream and become a doctor once he set foot on English soil. He traveled alone, and when he arrived in Odessa he had to wait to board the ship since it had been a severe winter and it was one of those rare instances when icebreaker assistance was required. The Black Sea coast is subject to freezing at times and they had to make arrangements to pull the ship out of the harbor.

Sitting in a small pub, trying to keep himself warm in his weather worn coat and drinking *pshenichnaya*—a variety of vodka, made with wheat instead of potatoes—he overheard a group of young Jewish men discussing their future plans in America. When they noticed him, they invited him to join them, not just at the table but also on their voyage to the New World. They were all slightly tipsy and boisterous, feeling very optimistic about their fates, and he was caught in their enthusiasm. America had always attracted him, and so he followed them to their ship that took sail within a short time without giving him another chance to rethink his sudden decision. By the time his head cleared, they were out of the harbor and all he could see was the lighthouse disappearing in the distance. Thus he did reach the New World, yet it was not North America as he had hoped for but, rather, South America—the port of Buenos Aires.

The hotel for the immigrants where he ended up was full of Russian Jews who had come to work in the agricultural colonies that the Baron de Hirsch had founded, hoping to find freedom from poverty and religious persecution, and a promising future.[1] Not knowing anybody in the city, feeling confused and lost, he decided to follow his countrymen to the *campo* and try to become a farmer. He hoped that in the future he could still pursue his dream and study to become a doctor. The hotel was humming all day long with families, some of them with many children, and even a few elderly people that had to be taken care of. Among them was a slender girl from Kamenets-Podolsk, the same town he came from, whom he admired in particular since she was not just beautiful but also assertive and cheerful in her ways. She was very young, barely fourteen years old, but they exchanged a few glances and it became love at first sight. The courtship was very short and they got married soon afterwards. In those days girls tied the knot very early; it was considered appropriate as long as the parents gave permission and authorized the wedding. He was six years her senior and was accepted with open arms by the family, who saw a great promise in his future.

He settled down with his wife in one of the colonies in the province of Buenos Aires. The foundation of Baron de Hirsch gave each of the settlers about hundred-and-fifty hectares of land (about three-hundred-and-seventy acres), and with their first born another hundred-and-fifty hectares were granted. The soil was rich but very compact and heavy, as it was virgin land, and the labor was backbreaking, particularly since he had no farming experience. However, he learned from some of the other settlers that had arrived from Russia who had had some agricultural background. Life was extremely hard but being young and full of hope, he did not lose spirit or desert the farm as many others, who faced failures, did in a relatively short amount of time. They lived in the *chacra*—their farm or property—in a clay hut, about twenty-five kilometers from the nearest village, where most people were Spaniards and Italians whose language they, at least initially, did not understand.[2] The settlers stuck together and kept their Jewish habits and customs. They continued speaking Yiddish and founded a school and a synagogue as soon as they could. They had to learn to work with bulls, and those who could afford it rode horses. Some years they had a good harvest and the conditions improved but at times calamity befell them in the shape of a plague of the locust.[3] Those destructive insects caused the heaviest damage to the crops; they came with the change of the winds and descended on the region in countless numbers like a dark menacing cloud. When it lifted, there was only devastation left. The Jewish settlers during those doomed days, when disaster cast its shadow on the fruits of their labor and nothing was left, felt like the inhabitants of ancient Israel when—as depicted in the Bible—the invasions of those merciless creatures caused the heaviest desolation to the land.

In time conditions improved somewhat and the family grew. The parents had to care for their nine children, all of whom participated in the life of the farm, helping as much as they could. At times there was also another kind of danger that they had to face—attacks by native Indians who came from afar to rob them of their possessions. They were not murderers and usually left them unharmed if they did not try to fight back; yet there was the case of a pregnant, young woman who would not part with some of the food she had stored in her kitchen and was killed struggling. However, that was a unique incident, since the Jews learned to accept the situation as long as they could not protect themselves. As the years passed and the settlements expanded, they regrouped in clusters of five to seven families, armed themselves, fought the invaders, and the raids stopped.

Time went by and the desire of becoming a doctor faded away. He was still a young man but the harsh conditions and his failing health, due to cancer of the stomach, shortened his life by many years, and when he died, his youngest child was only four years old. Yet, it was this son, by the name of Zeev, who kept alive the fervent wish of his father and became a doctor, thus fulfilling the dream the father had carried in his heart all his life.[4]

In 1928 the mother decided to move to Buenos Aires so that Zeev could attend high school. She shared his plans and knew that he needed to leave the colony in order to accomplish his dream. Two of his brothers were already in the city working as businessmen and the rest of the family continued living on the farm. Zeev always knew that he owed his degree to his mother for whom he felt not only great love but also deep respect. He became an obstetrician and, upon finishing his studies, left Buenos Aires in order to help a friend of his, who was a doctor as well, run a clinic in a remote village far from the capital. The name of the pueblo was Chos Malal, in the Province of Neuquen, in the Patagonian region of Argentina called the Cordillera del Viento. It was a small enclave of about two thousand very poor inhabitants that needed medical help badly. Zeev and his friend provided the village with compassionate care, but after a while Zeev decided to return to Buenos Aires, where he set up his own clinic and became very successful and respected as one of the best medics in town.

His life was blessed with a happy marriage and the birth of three sons who were bright and excelled in their studies. Zeev got involved in politics and for many years his services to the country were treasured and held in high regard. He held important government positions and also became an ambassador, which was a matter of great pride to his family, who never forgot their humble beginnings. He cultivated strong ties with Israel, visited the country many times, and created a bond that became even stronger as time went by. Life began changing drastically when Juan Peron rose to power in 1946; his anti-Semitic and fascist leanings caused the Jews a great amount of anxiety and the situation became worse as the years passed. However, Zeev continued caring for the patients in his clinic and devoting his time to political activities. He was jailed a few times because of his views, as well as for being Jewish. Once he was kept in jail for five months without being able to contact his family or his friends who, just like him, objected fiercely to the dictatorship and had refused to give in. He had been lucky initially and escaped an explosion caused by a bomb planted in their house, and even when their possessions were stolen, he still continued to endure. However, during the *golpe* in 1976, it became imperative for the whole family to leave the country in order to save their lives. The only one who refused to flee was the youngest son who was an avid follower of the revolution and stayed behind despite their pleas.

The family could not meet the young activist because of the danger involved and, thus, one day in order to say goodbye, just before their forced departure, Zeev ventured out to a place he knew his son frequented. After waiting for a few hours in the dark of night, with only the pale rays of the moon providing some light, he saw him coming out of a house. Challenging fate, he confronted him, urging him to reconsider and join them in their exodus. He never forgot the answer his son gave him before he crossed the street and disappeared down a narrow alley: "Alguno tiene que quedar para hacer la revolucion," he whispered, "somebody has to stay to make the revolution come true." Those were the last words Zeev heard from his son, who was killed one month after the family reached their safe haven in Venezuela.

Years have passed since they returned to Argentina from exile, and Zeev's heart aches whenever he thinks of his child. His son had inherited his grandfather's obstinate perseverance and strength of character to struggle under difficult circumstances and, in the end, also succumbed to a fate he could not overcome. Like his son, Zeev also loves the country he was born in and feels he has always been a good Argentinean, a devoted doctor, and a sincere Jew. His youngest boy was a fierce fighter, a hero who believed in ideals and in his mission to do the right thing. The silent prayer Zeev says in his heart every day is an ode to a departed son whom he loved dearly, admired intensely, and whom he will never see again.

Source Note

Based on an interview in Buenos Aires, March 2002. The interviewee wishes to remain anonymous.

Text Notes

1. Baron Maurice de Hirsch (1831–1896), a Jewish-German financier, dedicated his life and fortune to help East European Jews—toward the end of the nineteenth century—flee the pogroms and find a safe haven in Argentina and other countries. He believed that Jews could succeed in agricultural enterprises and founded many colonies, the most famous ones in the provinces of Buenos Aires and Santa Fe, with Moiseville leading the way. Initially these settlers had to fight many hardships but their successes were significant, although in time the population drifted to the cities. Today some of the land is still owned by Jews but most of the workers are gentiles.

2. The chacra is a spot where people cultivate plants—a field, yet it is more than just a place to the Andean people; it has a much broader meaning. It is symbolically the very heart of the regeneration of life and nature. Thus, for instance, the natives believe that a llama is "a chacra with legs", and the river where gold is found and panned is the "chacra of gold" (*http://nativenet.uthscsa.edu/archive/nl/9508/0073.html*).

3. Locust – a winged insect of the grasshopper family, which is extremely destructive and causes horrible devastation. The locust is mentioned many times

in the Bible as well as in other ancient historic documents, since these insects continually infested the Mediterranean area as well as Africa. They seem to be countless because they fly so close together and appear as a compact, moving, dark mass that advances slowly without stopping. They were eaten, boiled, or roasted and, at times, pounded and ground, mixed with water and flour, and made into cakes. The origin of this could lie in the fact that once these insects devastated the fields and all the vegetation was gone, there was nothing else left to eat.

4. Zeev – Hebrew name, meaning wolf.

The Cup and the Mug

Once there lived a small, elderly woman in a little house near Santiago. She had no family and very few friends left since she was very, very old. Nevertheless, she did not feel lonely because she had collected cups and mugs all her life and considered them company. She enjoyed looking at them, as they were all nicely placed and positioned in the big cupboard that dominated her diminutive kitchen. What a beautiful cupboard it was, made of shiny, dark wood and divided into many compartments! Over the years the old lady had filled them with different kinds of exclusive porcelain and ceramic cups and mugs. One could find the finest decorated coffee mugs as well as colored and glazed miniature teacups. There were pretty Bavarian cups with patterns of leaves in blue and silver. Some mugs were gold rimmed and had the insides glazed with milky-white, ruby-red, vibrant azure, or deep emerald colors. Next to the delicate white porcelain cups, there were charming country style ceramic mugs, stylish and sturdy, most of them in sky-blue, that depicted folk art from different regions of Chile and other countries in Latin America. Despite the bigger size, their shape was rounded and their handles felt comfortable to hold. They were meant for generous servings of one's favorite beverage.

On the higher shelves the old lady kept the most precious ones, treasures that she cherished and so did not use every day, just on special occasions such as her birthday or in loving memory of her husband, on their wedding anniversary. Those were antique cups, most of them in pastels—pink, lavender, baby-blue or light-green—and some of them with designs of delicate spring flowers, white fluffy cloud patterns, or even cheerful birds, and one or two with funny looking jesters. Her most exquisite one was a unique cup manufactured in Russia by the famous Lomonosov Porcelain factory, which had been founded in 1744 by the Emperor, Peter the Great. She had inherited it from her Jewish grandmother, who had come to Chile from Russia, and always treasured it greatly. But most of all she loved a small, pretty, hand-painted cup, which was adorned with a red poppy, a gift from her husband on their fiftieth anniversary, just a year before he passed away. She drank tea from it every day around five o'clock in the afternoon while she sat in her comfortable armchair in the kitchen and feasted her eyes on her treasures. She kept this little cup on the bottom shelf, hanging from a big hook that held it safely and comfortably, and which she could reach easily without having to stand on her toes. She was a very short, tiny lady and looked almost like a China doll fit to join her marvelous collection of porcelain cups in an exhibit. Next to her beloved poppy cup, there was a bigger mug that used to belong to her husband, hand stamped with a golden leaf and as elegant and classy as only a perfect mug could be. Over the years she had been so very careful that none of her cups had any chips or cracks, and she was very proud of the exceptional condition in which she kept them.

The old lady had no idea that the cupboard had a secret life of its own. She considered her collection inanimate, no doubt, but she was so very wrong about that. At night, the cupboard came to life; all of the cups and mugs exchanged conversations on different topics, mostly reminiscing, just like elderly people, about the places they came from and the good old days. Despite their desire to be used and serve the purpose for which they were created, they did not have any hard feelings for the old woman or hold any rancor for being kept just on display. They understood that her devotion and love kept them safe and out of danger. The favorite poppy cup had a great admirer in the golden-leafed mug that hung next to her. For a long time they had been considered a couple by the rest of the inhabitants of the cupboard. Some of the cups and mugs were envious of such a romantic, affectionate relationship, but it was crystal clear to all of them that this was a true love affair, as unique and everlasting as that between the old lady and her dear departed husband.

One quiet summer afternoon, the lady was resting in her armchair and drinking tea when suddenly she felt a jolt, as if the ground was moving under her, as if the room had begun dancing. She jumped up in fear and dropped the cup on the floor. It was just a mild earthquake that had affected the region and when the shaking subsided, she sat down once again and only then realized that her precious mug was on the floor—broken in two halves. She picked up the pieces with tears in her eyes and tried to put the two parts together again. There was no way she could drink from the cup anymore, she said to herself, and felt a deep pain as if a dear friend had died. She placed the cup gently on the countertop, too upset to discard it in the wastebasket, and sorrowfully retired to her bedroom. That night the whole cupboard mourned the passing of the poppy cup; well, everybody, that is, except the golden-leafed mug. He refused to accept her demise and insisted that there must be a way to bring her back. Nobody knows what really happened that dark and mysterious summer night, but in the morning the poppy cup was back, hanging on the hook with her parts nicely glued and mended together. Except for a very thin, hardly noticeable line, she was as good as new. Had a magician come to the help of the lovers? Had a witch flown by on her broom and seen from the open window the tragedy that was going on in the tiny kitchen? Nobody really knows . . .

The next afternoon when the old lady was pondering which one of the cups she should use for tea instead of her beloved poppy cup, she froze in her house shoes when she saw her hanging gracefully on the hook, shiny and colorful as always, as if telling her, "Here I am, here I am, please drink from me as you have always done!" And that is exactly what the old lady did!

Source Note

Based on an interview with Adriana Balter in Santiago, Chile, in March 2002. Adriana Balter is a musician who teaches at the University in Santiago. She cherishes the memory of her piano teacher, Elena Waiss, from whom she heard the cup and mug story for the first time. This is a fairytale that Elena Waiss, a well-known pianist and composer, used to tell her children and passed on to her students who told it to their children as well. It has been a favorite bedtime story. Fairytales were not common in Jewish households in Latin America, but sometimes Jews adopted a tale from the traditions of non-Jewish people and enjoyed them. Adriana Balter, whose predecessors were Russian and Polish Jews, remembers a few of that genre as well as some anecdotes about her relatives who emigrated to Argentina and Chile at the beginning of the twentieth century. She is also blessed with a mother, Tosca Balter, a writer and storyteller from whom she has inherited her imagination and artistic talent.

The Portrait

It hung in the living room, a large portrait placed in a very heavy wooden frame that the grandmother polished particularly carefully before Passover, when the whole house became like a showcase. The dark, shiny frame enhanced the white face of Baron de Hirsch, whose impressive moustache with its waxed, pointed ends frightened Norma whenever she happened to look at the picture.[1] The little girl was apprehensive despite the fact that the Baron did not look particularly menacing, just somewhat bossy and very determined. What bothered her most were his eyes that seemed to follow her wherever she was in the room, no matter what, even when other people were present. His upper lids covered the eyes partially and she hoped that the next time she looked at him, they would be fully closed and he would be sleeping. But the lids never closed completely, even when she imagined he had lowered them a bit, and he continued staring at her. She had the feeling that he knew exactly what she was thinking and, at times, doggedly refused to stay in the living room unless it was absolutely necessary. She did know that the wealthy Baron was a benefactor of the Jewish people and had even helped their relatives who lived in the colonies he had founded in various places in Argentina. Her grandparents often spoke of Baron de Hirsch and praised his kindness and willingness to assist those in need. However, she could not—even when she was older—fight the sensation that the man in the portrait was constantly seeking to impose his will on those who looked into his eyes.

Norma's maternal grandparents had come to Argentina from Russia in 1912, and she spent her childhood in their home, listening to many narratives her grandfather, who was a rabbi, told in Yiddish. He had many of those up his sleeve, some of them were quite amusing and unusual but for some reason he forbade Norma to retell the *narrishe* (silly) stories to anyone but members of the family. He had a beautiful voice and she recalls the lovely *cantitos* he often sang to her, the melodies that still bring tears to her eyes. Norma's grandfather was very respected by the members of his orthodox synagogue, and she was always very proud of him when the family went to the temple on Fridays, where from the women's balcony she watched him congregate with other important members of the community. She loved him with all her heart and the feeling was mutual. She was his favorite granddaughter and for her sake he was ready to overlook some of the rules that a religious person of his stature would have never accepted.

Once, on the last day of the Succoth festival—Simhat Torah (Rejoicing of the Torah)—the cycle of Torah readings was completed and a joyful procession, carrying one of the sacred scrolls, wound its way through the synagogue. Usually only men and boys took turns carrying the Torah, and a great sense of elation pervaded the congregation. Norma's grandfather did not let her ascend to the women's balcony that day but kept her with him and let her parade with the Torah for a while. The singing and dancing stopped and a deafening silence descended over the surprised people. A girl had been allowed to penetrate the exclusive male domain and perform a ritual forbidden to females; it had never happened before. The grandfather, though, was a *rebbe* and, thus, nobody dared to say a word. A few minutes later, the festivities continued and, after handing the scroll back to her grandfather, the proud girl joined the shocked yet delighted women on the balcony. That evening even Baron de Hirsch seemed pleased and less solemn to Norma and she was able to relax in the living room and disregard the portrait for the first time.

Norma grew up open-minded and as people-friendly as her grandfather had been. She encountered anti-Semitism even while she was a youngster attending a secular school in downtown Buenos Aires. She learned to accept it, handle it, and fight it, and her life became bearable once she realized that there were many decent and courageous people in the world regardless of their religious affiliation. She opened her heart, particularly to those she admired. When Norma was twelve years old, sometime during the Peron regime. she had a friend, Maria Esther, whose family had escaped the Spanish Civil War. Maria, who was about Norma's age, was a Catholic and wore her favorite jewelry, a large cross, around her neck. The two girls became close friends and very attached to each other. Every day Jewish children were ordered to spend their time waiting outdoors while all the others attended religious sessions. One day, when the headmaster ordered the Jews to get out, Maria Esther followed her banished friend into the courtyard. The austere teacher told her that she was not the one who was supposed to leave, but Maria Esther, holding on to her golden cross, faced the teacher and, looking straight into her eyes, told her that she was not interested in their religious studies and preferred to join her "sister" in the courtyard.

Years later, as a married woman, Norma and her engineer husband moved with their family—they had three lovely daughters—from Buenos Aires to the seaside resort of Mar de la Plata, about four hundred kilometers south of the capital. Mar del Plata offers its inhabitants one of the most beautiful sceneries in the world. The ample, fine sand beaches stretch over a long distance caressing the ocean and the mild climate is enjoyable all year round. Mountain ranges frame Mar de la Plata from afar. The beauty of their new home, as well as the many interesting landmarks, charmed Norma and her family. Norma's romantic spirit was fascinated particularly by the legend of Torreón del Monje (Monk's Tower), a castle that was built on a terrace overlooking the sea. It was not just the beauty of the scenery that captivated her heart but also the mystery of the legend. She sympathized with the unhappy soldier who, upon losing his beloved, had locked himself inside the tower for the rest of his life and whose ghost was supposed to roam around the structure on moonlit nights. But then, she never lacked imagination and often visualized and understood things other people were not aware of. The portrait of Baron de Hirsch was not among her belongings; it had been given to an uncle who was a baker and who cherished the exceptional painting, and, in a way, she did miss it because it reminded her of her childhood.

In 1962, when they moved into town, there was a small Jewish congregation in Mar de la Plata that consisted of about two hundred families that kept very close together. They lived dispersed among the gentiles but followed their cultural tradition and sent their children to a Jewish school. Holidays were always a special time for them, particularly Passover, and the preparations by the small community were always meticulous and intense. When Passover was about to begin, the year Norma and her family arrived there, many of the non-Jewish families amongst whom they lived showed a lot of interest and curiosity. One day a neighbor innocently asked Norma whether it was true that Jews needed blood to bake their matzah. This inquiry caused Norma a lot of distress and she went at once to see the rabbi to express her frustration, anger, and sense of helplessness. The young rabbi was a very wise man and decided to handle the problem in a rather unconventional way. He summoned the whole congregation and they agreed to celebrate the Passover holiday on the sidewalk in one particular area in town. They were granted permission by the city hall and sent out an invitation to all the neighbors. The rituals and ceremonies were performed according to Jewish conservative rules and explained to the guests who, at the end, were very pleased and expressed their enjoyment and satisfaction at finding out what Passover was really all about. The rabbi and the congregation continued this practice each holiday for one year. Thus they not only averted a potential crisis that could have led to anti-Semitism based on ignorance, but also gained many new friends, some of whom became addicted to Jewish cooking. The gentile community accepted them after that with open arms and respected their customs and habits. The Jews were very much at home in Mar de la Plata; they felt a genuine sense of belonging, which they craved for and were able to pass on to their children.

Norma often reminisces about those days in Mar de la Plata, where she had been very happy, and in a soft voice hums the melody "Casta Diva" from Bellini's opera, *Norma*, which she loves. Jokingly, she comments that if the portrait of Baron de Hirsch had been hanging on one of the walls in her sunny home in Mar de la Plata, his severe gaze would have softened considerably—she is quite positive about it—and, in any case, it would have not bothered her anymore.

Source Note

Based on an interview with Norma Salomon de Malamud in Buenos Aires, March 2002.

Text Notes

1. For more information about Baron de Hirsch, please refer to the tale "Ode to a Dead Son."

Virgin Mary

Rachel had never seen Sudele but felt she knew her well based on the stories she had heard from her father. Sudele was a strong, young mule born in Bessarabia a long time ago. She belonged to Rachel's grandparents, who owned a small plant that manufactured fermented drinks. Sudele was a very clever animal and followed the orders she was given in good faith, and without complaining or putting up tantrums. This was indeed quite commendable since the labor she had to endure was not easy and extremely monotonous and boring. She was tethered every morning to a millstone and had to tread around and around endlessly in circles while the grain was being ground as the first step in making *kvass*, which was the favorite drink of many people in the region.[1] God knows what Sudele was thinking as she obediently walked on her circular journey to nowhere. Yet, she most probably was not aware of the different kinds of grains that were used, such as wheat, rye, barley, and buckwheat, to produce one of the national drinks of Russia. Every evening, though, she enjoyed tasting some of the finished product, especially the apple-flavored kvass. Even the very low alcoholic content made Sudele somewhat tipsy and happy but mainly promoted good sleep, which left her refreshed and full of energy come next morning. Rachel's father had felt a lot of affection for the little mule, and Rachel, who never tired of listening to his tales, shared his sentiments and always had a soft spot in her heart for any mule or donkey she happened to encounter.

Rachel's father and two of his brothers had arrived in Brazil in the early 1920s. He had left behind the small shtetl in Bessarabia with its Jewish shopkeepers, such as shoemakers, bakers, butchers, coachmen, blacksmiths, and other artisans and merchants, who were the main life force of the shtetl. As much as he missed his family and admired the Jewish community there, where people always had to rely on each other, he wanted to find something different in the New World, a unique experience that would offer him a good life and safety. Being of an inquisitive and bold nature, the three brothers decided, before settling down in any one place in Brazil, to tour the Amazonia looking for adventures. There existed no well-defined transportation system in those days. Thus they sailed on boats along the rivers, walked for long periods of time, and rode donkeys for days without end. It took them a year and a half to return to Sao Paulo, the place where they had begun their odyssey. Rachel never heard the amazing tales she might have expected from her father since the journey into the wilderness of Brazil had ended in tragedy, and nobody wanted to bring it up, even after years of silence. All Rachel knew was that one of her uncles had died. He had been bitten by a snake and, despite the fact that his brothers tried to suck the venom out of his affected leg and even cut off a piece of flesh to get rid of the poison, they could not save him and he passed away in their arms. The desperate brothers, grieving and desolate, had no choice but to bury their sibling in a spot, somewhere in the depths of the jungle, knowing they would never again be able to find his grave. Upon their arrival in Sao Paulo, they erected a headstone in his honor in the local cemetery and felt some relief since it was the only way to express their love for him, the only tangible means to keep his memory recorded.

Rachel's father settled down in the small mining town of Sao Joao del Rei, in Minas Gerais, a state in the center of the country without any access to the sea. In the early eighteenth century, gold was discovered in the region and the first settlement was founded.[2] As time went by, ornate landmarks designed by the best architects of the era graced the town. When Rachel's father made his home in Sao Joao del Rei, there were many beautiful pastel-painted colonial homes in the area that belonged to prominent families, some of which still stand today. In time, the small town became enchanting with its cobblestone streets and sidewalks and a winding stream that crosses the locality, and crowned by many churches that were raised as signs of Christian devotion by the inhabitants of the region. When the gold ran out and mining activity ended at the beginning of the nineteenth century, ranching and trade took its place and became quite successful. Carpets manufactured locally became particularly well known and the textile industry continues to thrive today. The landscape around the town has changed considerably since those gold mining days; mowed fields have replaced densely wooded areas and animals such as wild marmosets and lemurs, close relatives of better known small monkeys that frequented the rain forests of the past, are hard to find.

One of the most interesting buildings is the large Church of Sao Francisco de Assis. It was built in 1774 and superbly decorated with statues created by Brazil's famous eighteenth century sculptor Antonio Francisco Lisboa, who is affectionately known by his nickname of Aleijadinho or "the little cripple." The brilliant artist was indeed disfigured, most probably because of leprosy, but was able to create unbelievably beautiful works of art despite his handicap. As a young child, Rachel was very much impressed by the majestic, gilded church and the round towers that were incorporated by the artist into the design. She often marveled at the exuberantly decorated portal featuring the Virgin Mary with a crown on her head and the sweet cherubs that kept her company. Maybe it was already at that time, well before she became a pupil in the local convent, that she began to feel an affinity with the mother of Jesus.

Rachel's parents had married within a month after they met for the first time and their marriage was a life-long attachment, filled with love and bliss. Rachel likes to dwell on their story, which she laments ended in illness and their demise within just three days of each other, as if they could not tolerate being separated and had to continue together their journey into the other world. Jewish life was celebrated within the family and the holidays were observed; yet Rachel was sent at a very early age to a convent that was renowned for its secular curriculum. Rachel's parents wanted her to benefit from the excellent education the school provided but did not anticipate then the rift it would create between them and their daughter in the years to come. The nuns did not impose their religion on students that were of a different faith, but the kindness and the attention they showered so lovingly had a very strong effect on the small children. Rachel adored the nuns and felt very much at home within the walls of the convent. It was not an austere, gloomy place but rather a habitat full of light, laughter, and joy. She admired the many statues of the Virgin

Mary that decorated the convent and the churches in town. During this period, as well as later in life, she was keenly aware of a sense of awe and uplifted spirits whenever she visited Christian places of worship. In the Cathedral Basilica de Nossa Senhora das Pilar, she gasped when she saw the amazing interior with Rococo pillars, the ceiling painted with religious scenes, the beautiful tiled floor, carved angels, and fancy curlicues. The etchings in the stone steps of the Igreja de Nossa Senhora das Merces and the artistry of the woodcarvings in all the churches made Baroque art one of her passions in life.

One year, the nuns were busy setting up a beautiful nativity scene for the Christmas holidays and preparing a play depicting the journey of Mary and Joseph to Bethlehem and the birth of Christ. The girl that was supposed to portray the Virgin became ill and Rachel volunteered to play the part. She was very excited and felt that, in a way, it was meant to happen because of her admiration for the beauty and serenity of the mother of Jesus. Rachel was a very lovely child and looked captivating in her long dress, sitting on the little donkey that the sisters had rented for the play. She was thrilled with the small animal that stood patiently for a while but not for too long. For some reason, he wanted to walk in circles all around the yard where they were rehearsing, and looked upset and brayed sadly when the nuns prevented that and made him stand in one place. Rachel sensed that somehow the little donkey had to be a reincarnation of her father's loyal friend in Bessarabia, and gently scratched him around the neck, whispering the name Sudele into his long ears. It worked like magic; as soon as the donkey heard the name, he calmed down and stood still, at least for a while. Rachel's father was very amused when she told him about the donkey and complimented his daughter on her vivid imagination. Neither of her parents objected to the daughter playing the Virgin Mary; they just saw it as a manifestation of one of her many talents and had no idea how deeply it affected her.

As time went by Rachel felt very confused and guilty. She loved the nuns deeply and did not know how to deal with her inner friction. She felt remorseful, being Jewish and aware of her people's history and fate, to be so devoted to the ideals of the Christian church and the Virgin Mary in particular. She tried to fight her bewilderment and came to the conclusion that the feeling of blame would fade away and eventually dissipate were she to convert to Christianity. In a way, she resented her parents for having sent her to the convent and creating the dilemma for her. She knew they would not allow her to follow her heart. She felt unhappy and despondent, but finally confided in them and tried to explain what she believed in. They were not just surprised but really shocked and horrified to learn how their daughter felt and what her intentions were. It was simply unthinkable for them and, thus, at the age of fifteen, Rachel's parents moved the family to Sao Paulo so she could get used to life in an established Jewish community. This was done not only to prevent her from converting but also to make it less likely that she would end up marrying a non-Jew when she grew up. At first Rachel felt rebellious and distressed but, being basically of an outgoing and positive disposition, soon found new friends who helped her overcome her ordeal. Over time she adjusted well and learned to appreciate the ancient heritage into which she had been born.

Many years have passed since then and Rachel feels comfortable with the faith of her people. She is very proud of the fact that many prominent figures in Brazilian society have come from Jewish stock. When she visits Sao Joao del Rei once in a while, she becomes somewhat sentimental looking at the churches she used to be so attached to, but the confusion and the guilt are gone. She has remained, nevertheless, a very open-minded person and believes in her heart that goodness in people is what really matters and that there is no basic difference among them as long as there is faith.

Source Note

Based on an interview with Rachel Rosenblum in Sao Paulo, Brazil, in March 2002. Rachel is a prominent translator, proficient in many languages, and a good friend of Goan Thong Yo, who is a dear friend of the author.

Text Notes

1. *Kvass* or *Kwass*, a Russian word for "leaven," an alcoholic drink popular in Russia and Eastern Europe, is made by a simultaneous acid and alcoholic fermentation of various grains or old rye-bread (a viable option) to which fruits

or sugars have been added. It has been a favorite drink since the sixteenth century, initially a domestic production, mostly a poor man's form of beer. The beverage often has an opaque, amber color and is considered mainly a summer drink—vodka being preferred by most in the cold of the winter. Nowadays, it is made commercially in large towns, has become superior to the homemade brew, and often flavored with apples, raspberries, or mint due to its bittersweet taste.

2. The discovery of gold in Brazil – Initially more important than the small town of Sao Joao del Rei, there was another one, only a short distance away, called Ouro Preto—meaning black gold—that became the first capital of Minas Gerais. Many Portuguese adventurers and Paulistas (people from Sao Paulo), called bandeirantes, descended on the area even before 1700. Legend tells us that a thirsty man, drinking from a brook in that location, found some black stones which he kept and later discovered that when cracked they contained the precious metal. The coloring of the stone was caused by the iron oxide in the soil. Gold was also abundant in nearby Sao Joao del Rei and in the foothills of the neighboring mountains. In addition to gold, the area is also known for its exquisite pink topaz (*http://members.tripod.com.br; http://www.pacificislandtravel.com*).

An Orange On Board
the LUSITANIA

One day in the summer of 1912, on the lower deck of the swiftest ship in the world sailing towards America, there stood a young girl holding in both her hands a beautiful orange. She held it carefully, admiring the intense, bright color of the fruit, and, lifting it close to her nostrils, inhaled the sweet scent over and over again. So absorbed was she in enjoying the fruit that she did not seem to pay too much attention to the boundless ocean that spread all around her. It was a beautiful, calm day; the light sea breeze playfully fluffed up her dark, long hair, and some of the passengers looked with curiosity at the frail, young girl who seemed to be oblivious to everything except the shiny object in her hands. It was the first orange that she had ever had! It was a miracle to behold, not to be eaten, at least not for a while. She was a Jewish lass from a tiny Ukrainian village who had been very lucky to have the opportunity to cross the ocean on board the mighty *Lusitania*.[1] The ship was gigantic, no doubt, and, although she slept in a third class cabin and ate in the huge third class dining saloon, she had caught a glimpse of the glamour of the upper decks and felt she was experiencing a strange, unbelievable dream. She had mistakenly wandered into the first-class dining area, which was so huge that it occupied two decks and was capped by a shiny dome with stained-glassed depictions. Amazed and terrified, she had run into the wrong room and realized at once that it was a regal suite, designed exclusively for the wealthiest passengers. When she finally made her way back, stumbling in and out of some fancy chambers with heavy ornate arches and pillars, she found refuge in her simple quarters, crawled into the berth, covered herself with a blanket, and stayed there until the trembling subsided and she was able once again to get up and find her way to the lower deck.

She wanted to be alone with the orange while her brothers were still in the dining room, enjoying the bounty of food, such as they had never seen in their lifetime. She thought of their hardships, of the cold freezing winter days, of the deadly influenza that had devastated the village and killed six of her siblings. She saw her mother's ashen face as she gave away two of her little brothers to a couple of wealthy people from the city who had come to buy children they could not have on their own. Her mother had sold them to save their lives; although she had had eighteen of them, she could not forget those that were given away. She had mourned their departure, despite the fact that she felt no remorse, believing in her heart that she had saved them from the evil eye of the disease and snatched them away from the jaws of death. How fortunate they had been to have a kind-hearted, rich, and generous relative in America who had sent them money for the trip and promised to help them get settled in the New World! Her mother had chosen her and two of her older brothers to undertake the voyage, with the hope that the rest of the family would be able to join them in the future.

The *Lusitania* was sailing at top speed, the ship was not far from the shores of North America, and the passage was almost at its end. The young girl carefully placed the lovely orange in one of the inner pockets her mother had sown into her ample dress. The cautious woman had warned her daughter not to take any chances and to hide anything of value within the safe folds of her garment. She would have loved to have shown the orange to her mother, let her feel the smooth skin of the fruit, and sense the zesty aroma. She smiled as she recalled her mother telling the children one of Shalom Aleichem's stories about the boy who had eaten an orange on Rosh Hashanah, despite the fact that it was not permitted, and how he had been punished for his disobedience.[2] In the old country, oranges were regarded as almost sacred since they came from the Holy Land and, as such, were considered to be unique, only to be looked at, as if there was something magical about them. She was elated that she had one all to herself, and maybe she would get one more before the end of their journey. In America, she had heard, oranges were plentiful and inexpensive. She could hardly believe her good fortune!

Suddenly everybody on the deck was shouting and pointing to the horizon, and as she made an effort to see what people were so excited about, the girl saw far away the outline of the Statue of Liberty. People were screaming joyfully and hugging each other; the commotion and the excitement were intense. She stood transfixed for a while and felt tears streaming down her face. She knew what the Statue of Liberty symbolized and what she was hoping for once she entered the gates of the New World. Slowly she pulled out the orange from the depths of her pocket and sank her fingers into the deep, shiny skin of the fruit. She peeled it carefully, saving the fragrant rind in the deepest pouch of her dress. She spread the sweet sections of the fruit in the palm of her hand and slowly savored the heavenly taste of her very first orange . . .

Source Note

Based on an interview with Lezak Shallat in Santiago, Chile, March 2002. Lezak Shallat was born in the United States and is a writer and editor in Santiago, Chile. It was her maternal grandmother who had her first taste of an orange on board the *Lusitania* as she sailed towards a new beginning in the New World.

Text Notes

1. The *Lusitania*, a British passenger ship, was sunk off the Irish Coast by a German submarine on May 7, 1915. Close to two thousand people lost their lives, among them one hundred and twenty-eight American citizens. This tragedy precipitated the entry of the United States of America into World War I (*http://www.pbs.org/lostliners/lusitania.html*).

2. Shalom Aleichem (1859–1916: "Peace be upon you"), pseudonym of the famous Russian Yiddish writer Shalom Rabinowitz.

Where the Navel is Buried

A giant Kapok tree spreads its immense canopy over a large area, just as its enormous plank roots extend out from the trunk in all directions.[1] This marvelous tree, which is also called the Silk Cotton tree, is mostly at home in the rain forest, yet it thrives miraculously in the arid soil of the island of Curacao where it was transplanted about four hundred years ago. The Caiquetios, a tribe of peace loving Arawak Indians, had come to the island from neighboring Venezuela, unwilling to engage continually with rival bellicose tribes. They had brought the tree as a remembrance of the place they had been forced to leave and cherished it as a symbol of their former homeland. The Caiquetios did not enjoy the haven they found for long since, within a few years after their first contact with white men, they either succumbed to diseases or were forced into slavery. Today, only traces of their culture are visible at some archeological sites such as rock paintings and petroglyphs in the caves of Curacao and other nearby islands. Yet, the Kapok tree, which twice a year releases a multitude of cottony fluff from its seedpods and covers the ground with a white blanket as pure as snow, is perhaps the best memorial these first known inhabitants of the island could have asked for.

Curacao, a part of the Dutch Antilles, has had a rather tumultuous history over the centuries, ever since either Alonso de Ojeda, one of Columbus' officers, or Amerigo Vespucci, himself, discovered it in the year 1499. The Dutch conquered the island in 1638 and transformed it into a small-scale version of Holland. They were very tolerant and liberal and, thus, many people who had been persecuted in Europe for one reason or another found refuge in Curacao. Over the years, despite many upheavals, Sephardic Jews, originally from Spain and Portugal, settled down in Curacao, prospered, and became a very important element in the economy, politics, and culture of the island. They became attached to it and in time felt that true to its meaning in

Portuguese—Coracao—the *heart* of the Antilles, it became also the center of their world.[2] There were many business opportunities that enabled the Jews to make a good living due to the island's strategic location in the Caribbean. Yet another advantage was the year-round warm weather of the island, light rainfall, sunshine with cool temperatures because of the trade winds, and low danger of destructive storms since it lies well below the hurricane belt. The dry climate is very beneficial for people with certain ailments such as rheumatism and pulmonary diseases. Curacao's crystalline beaches, the well-protected coral reefs, and the abundance of wildlife added to the charm of the island and also inspired its inhabitants in their artistic endeavors.

The Jews are very loyal to the Dutch House of Orange and the Queen whom they admire and love. They are grateful for the three hundred and fifty years of freedom in Curacao and for the help that the Royal House provided their ancestors in Holland. During the Torah services at the synagogue, they add a thanksgiving prayer in Portuguese to honor the House of Orange and ask for its good fortune. They mention the name of Queen Beatrix, her mother, Juliana, and her son, Prince William Alexander, as well and the governor of their island. This is unique to the Sephardic Jews of Curacao. Their connection is with the House of Orange mainly, not necessarily to the culture of Holland or the Dutch language, which is the official tongue of the island.[3] Many of them travel to Holland on business or for graduate studies. They also visit a memorial built in honor of a local hero by the name of George Levy Maduro. This young man was studying in Holland during World War II and fought as a lieutenant in the Dutch army. He participated in many battles, was captured at the end, and perished in the Dachau concentration camp just before its liberation. In his honor a miniature village was built close to The Hague as a testimonial.

A channel provides the entrance to Willemstad, the capital of Curacao, from the Caribbean Sea and divides the town in two parts. A floating bridge, which is swung out of the way to enable ship traffic, connects the two parts of the town. The architecture is Dutch and very colorful. Since their arrival in Curacao the Jews were involved in the maritime industry, excelled at it, and prospered. Later on they pursued other enterprises such as trade, banking, and insurance, and have continued to do so into the present. The old Jewish community of Curacao, revered for its illustrious past in Spain, Portugal, and Holland, is well known for Beth Haim, its ancient cemetery that goes back to 1659, as well as for Mikveh Israel-Emmanuel, which was consecrated in 1742 and is the oldest synagogue in existence in the New World. They also have a good relationship with the other groups on the island whom they accepted with grace and understanding and helped in numerous ways.[4] Many Antilleans who come from a variety of different backgrounds are connected to Jewish procreators. They use their fathers' Jewish names, are proud of their heritage, and contribute vastly to the community not just with their talents and devotion but with their customs and habits as well.

The Yaya, or nanny, has always been a blessing to the Jewish community of Curacao.[5] A member of the Afro-Caribbean community, mostly a descendant of the slaves, she was hired by the master of the Jewish household and became the second mother to his children. The Yaya cared for them day and night and had a strong influence on their upbringing. The birth mother was usually busy with her social duties and, either because of her standing in society or at times for medical reasons, would not deal with the menial tasks of the household. The mansions of the wealthy were built in a rambling ranch style, and needed a great many laborers to maintain them—such as cooks, gardeners, cleaning maids, washerwomen, and errand boys. These servants were trained to do their jobs properly and the Yaya was the most trusted and beloved one. Often, she would follow the grown children to their own homesteads and continue taking care of the new offspring. When the Yaya became old or ill, the family provided for her until the end of her days. Although knowledgeable in the Jewish way of life and respectful of their habits and customs, the Yaya exposed the children to a very different world, mainly through her stories, which came from her own African tradition and had a strong effect on the youngsters. The well-known tales of the sly spider Nanzi or Compa Nanzi were basically the only folktales and fables the Jewish children heard in their childhood.

The Nanzi stories were usually short, anthropomorphic, and had moral overtones.[6] Much was also left to the imagination so that the children could ask questions and even add their own little twists to the tales. Thus, the Yaya was also a teacher who provided not only entertainment but taught them the difference between right and wrong, what is courageous and what is cowardly, and exposed them to a different culture, language, and knowledge of many kinds of animals, birds, and plants that were to be found on the island. She introduced them to the innumerable species of cacti, applied the slimy sap of the Aloe plants on their cuts and bruises, and warned them not to touch the hairy leaves of the nettle plants that secrete a poison that causes itching and swelling. She also prevented them from eating the manchineel (manzalina), a certain variety of small, green, and yellow round apples that are poisonous and whose juice can irritate the skin. The Yaya protected the youngsters from mosquitoes and calmed their fears when they encountered an iguana, the king of the Curacao reptiles, which despite its dragon-like ferocious look is in fact quite shy. She explained the difference between a species of geckos and bats. The geckos have bulging eyes and translucent skin, are able to climb walls, and, at times, are to be found hanging head down inside a closet, just like bats that abound in the caves of Curacao, but are not hurtful. The Yaya instilled in the children an admiration for the many native birds of the island, such as the brown and white sandpipers, long legged egrets, and the occasional flamingos that congregated in shallow waters. No wonder that the Yaya became such an important member of the Jewish family in Curacao; she did so many things: she entertained, informed, instructed, and mainly gave the children her loyal, loving care and undivided attention.

Despite her benevolent nature, the Yaya also told the children many ghost tales that often frightened them and, in the long run, made them superstitious, but these stories were, in fact, educational and entertaining as well, and a part of the daily life in Curacao that could not be ignored. There are hardly any Jewish ghost tales that deal with the same kind of spirits and apparitions that are typical of the Caribbean folklore; nevertheless, there is one that has, no doubt, been influenced by the local lore.

There was a house built on a desolate plot that faced a hill where there were many caves; the rest of the area had remained undeveloped for a long time. A huge black cross was painted on the door of this house in which a Jewish family lived. Nobody knows why but the inhabitants of that house were possibly frightened and tried to prevent evil spirits that supposedly lived in the caves from entering their home. They believed that such vicious forces could not be Jewish.

Some of the local superstitions became an integral part of Jewish everyday life. A few are also based on Biblical beliefs and traditional customs that were carried over from the past. When a baby is born, one has to watch over it for eight days to prevent the African spirit, Eze, from snatching the child. The color blue is considered effective in keeping away Eze as well as other vicious spirits. A chalky substance (called *blous* in the commonly used Papiamentu language) is smeared on the crown of the babies' heads and the soles of their feet. This is a custom reminiscent of the precautions taken by Jews to prevent the wicked Lillith from kidnapping the newborn. Until the age of three or four, the child wears an amulet, a *hamsah*, local beads of some sort, or a blue-dyed pattern on the back of its clothes so that the evil spirit will see it and retreat. Later on the amulets would not be needed since the child is expected to have gained enough fortitude and stamina to fight off the curses without the support of such talismans. The other inhabitants have their own ways of protecting themselves from evil spirits and are mostly not aware of or, perhaps, not interested in the Jewish customs, beliefs, and holiday rituals. On the other hand, the Jews are not only knowledgeable about the celebrations of the Curacao people but participate in the New Year holiday and other popular festivals.

The Jewish population enjoys the hearty local cuisine, including the typical sweets. These delicacies can be purchased in kiosks on street corners or in bakeries. The Curacao Liquor distilled by the Jews is a favorite product and so is a special brand of coffee that has a story behind it. The fame of the Capriles' coffee goes back to an ancestor of the Capriles family who was a renowned Jewish medic. A long time ago, Dr. Capriles, who practiced aboard a ship, arrived at the island, and as soon as the vessel anchored he was summoned to help the ailing daughter of the ruler of Curacao. After he took care of the young girl and before returning to the ship, Dr. Capriles was offered a cup of coffee that happened to be too hot for him to drink. Thus, he politely blew and blew on the hot beverage to cool it since it was taking too long and he was in a hurry. It so happened that before he had a chance to finish the drink, his ship suddenly exploded and everybody on board perished. Dr. Capriles had been saved thanks to the steaming cup of coffee and since that day, when a person gets a cup of coffee that is too hot to drink, it is referred to as the "Capriles coffee." The slave who had served the coffee to the doctor was granted freedom as he had saved not only the doctor's life but also enabled the continuation of his lineage. Today, this specific brand of coffee is sold in different locations on the island.

Curacao is a place of many wonders, where the common and the unusual intermingle, and the eerie at times appears out of nowhere. In particular, the sea is a world that holds many marvels in its depths. One of them is a strange phosphorescence that creeps out of the water and glows in the dark of night.[7] The gleam spreads around the shores of the island and illuminates big areas on the water as well as on land. The brilliant light embraces numerous trees that emit an unparalleled magical green aura of their own as if hiding an underground secret. In reality, many of them actually do cradle an incredible buried treasure. The interred keepsakes are symbolical and in a way more precious than any gem. Those are the umbilical cords, the navels of the infants born on the island, that have been buried under trees, a Jewish custom that is meant to emphasize the deep love and everlasting tie the people feel toward the place they call home.[8]

Source Note

Based on an interview in Curacao, in March 2002, with Etsel (Papy) Jesurun, Charles Gomes-Casseres, Michele Russel-Capriles, Lucille Berry-Haseth, Rosemary de Paula, Diane Henriquez, Joan Capriles, and Eunice Delvalle.

Text Notes

1. The Kapok tree (*Ceiba pentandra*) is a tropical tree that can reach the height of a hundred and fifty feet. The billowing canopy of the tree serves as

home to many varieties of birds and other animals, such as bats and several kinds of insects. It is the most venerated tree in Central America. The ancient Mayans believed that it stood at the center of the earth and served as a connection with the heavens since the souls of the departed would ascend along its long spreading branches. Also, according to another ancient legend, the first man was created from its thick, heavy trunk. The particular tree mentioned in the story can be viewed at Hofi Pastor, a hundred and twenty-nine acre protected park with many beautiful, exceptional trees in the island of Curacao (*http://www.ceiba.org/ceiba.htm*).

2. The origin of the name of the island has many versions. One is that a cartographer sketched the island in the shape of a heart, "Corazon" (in Spanish), as it was in the center on the Antilles. Another theory is that Amerigo Vespucci, on his way to South America, was forced to leave behind on the shore of the island a group of sick sailors who suffered from scurvy. He was positive they would die and, upon his return a year later, was very surprised to find them recovered and healthy. He came to the conclusion that something on the island had cured them, and, hence, he called it "Curacao," from the Portuguese word "to cure." The Caiquetios were very tall people and, thus, the Spaniards also nicknamed the place "La Isla de Los Gigantes," meaning "The Island of the Giants." The Lesser Antilles was also named "Islas Inútiles," which meant "Useless Islands" because no precious metals or natural riches were found. The harbor and the location of the island were always the island's most important assets (*http://www.globalxs.nl/home/j/jasonfd/curacao.htm*; *http://www.nelsal.com/History.htm*).

3. The languages – Dutch has been the official language of Curacao since 1634. Portuguese, Spanish, and English also serve as means of communication. Papiamentu, which is a mixture of Dutch, Portuguese, Spanish, some English, and African languages, as well as words preserved from the ancient inhabitants of the island, is widely prevalent as a vernacular and was spoken by the Jews around as early as the year 1750. One of the oldest documents preserved in that language is a love letter sent by a Portuguese Jewess to her lover that dates back to 1775.

4. A group of Ashkenazi Jews settled down in Curacao in the twentieth century and also became successful in their endeavors. Some of them came to the island after the outbreak of World War II, fleeing from the Nazi persecution. They established their own synagogue and have a good relationship with members of the Sephardic congregation. Over the years many of the Sephardic Jews moved on to other Caribbean islands. There is a large group from Curacao now living in Panama, where they have become very prominent.

5. The Yaya – The name is most probably onomatopoeic since Yayas used to

talk continuously and tell stories, most probably based on a Cajun dialect in which it means "talking all the time or at the same time with others." The word is used in many other cultures as well.

6 Nanzi stories – The famous spider tales originally come from the Ashanti Africans of Ghana. The word "anansi," meaning "spider," is symbolic of a sly and naughty arachnid that takes advantage of simple-minded and innocent creatures that, nevertheless, come out unharmed at the end of each story (*http://65.113.91.126/mls_website/AnduzeThesis/Storyteller*).

7. Phosphorescence – The emission of light from the sea is a phenomenon that occurs when the phosphorescent plankton is disturbed, causing the water to be illuminated. This can also be caused by stimulation, such as when an oar hits the waves or when the wind ripples the surface of the sea.

8. The Umbilical Cord – In other Caribbean islands, such as Haiti, the umbilical cord of a newborn is also saved, dried, and planted in the ground together with the pit from a fruit tree. The tree that grows out of it becomes the property of the child and, symbolically, its guardian angel. It is a good sign when the tree is healthy and flourishes but a bad omen if, for some reason, it withers, becomes crooked, or dies; see Diane Wolkstein, *The Magic Orange Tree and Other Haitian Folktales* (New York: Schoken Books, 1997), 14.

The Encounter

Washington arrived at Juan Santamaria International Airport in San Jose, Costa Rica, at dusk. It had been a long flight, just as many he had undertaken in the past, but this one was a trip he would never forget. This time he had not watched the descent into the green and beautiful valley in which the capital of Costa Rica is located, nor did he recall with amusement Columbus' mistake in naming the place Costa Rica—The Rich Coast—assuming that there was a lot of gold in the newly discovered land. Columbus found very little of the precious metal there, yet the magical landscape of Costa Rica has since those early days served as a major attraction to tourists and been a golden source of income to its friendly native people.[1]

No, he did not ponder about anything of that kind while the plane was approaching its destination, but with his eyes closed lived again through a unique experience that would remain with him the rest of his life.

He had begun his flight in Lima, Peru. While he was waiting to board the plane at the Jorge Chavez International Airport, he noticed a bearded man wearing a tall, black hat and a long dark coat, as is the habit of religious Jews. The man was sitting in one of the chairs in the waiting area, his eyes closed and his body relaxed. He seemed to be tired and either resting or even sleeping, and there was something very peaceful and soothing about his appearance. It looked as if he was dozing off in his own home, unaware of his surroundings and oblivious to the constant noise. Nevertheless, his eyelids flickered and he opened them under the intense gaze of Washington, who for some reason was fascinated by him. Being Jewish himself, Washington had seen many orthodox Jews in his lifetime and they had never attracted his attention in particular. He was quite surprised at his own reaction and felt somewhat embarrassed to realize that the stranger had noticed his interest in him.

Washington, who was born in Montevideo, Uruguay, had always

been aware of his Polish Jewish roots. His parents had kept a conservative home and he grew up with the name Isaac, following Jewish tradition. The secular appellation of Washington was very popular in those days and had been suggested by a family friend at the time of his birth. As he grew up in Chile, where his family later settled down, as a young man studying for a law degree and involved in politics of the times, he drifted away from Judaism and did not feel the need to observe it the way his family had done. Yet, that day at the Lima airport, he suddenly felt a tremendous urge to approach the bearded man and speak in Yiddish. He had not spoken the language for years. He had never, ever addressed anybody in the tongue of his forefathers since he had left home and did not miss it at all, but at that moment—looking into the somber eyes of the stranger— he somehow felt compelled to do so.

He approached the stranger and greeted him in Yiddish. He felt relieved when the man smiled and asked him to sit down next to him. Washington was quite comfortable telling him about his unusual urge to speak Yiddish when he had noticed him dozing off in the chair. The man listened carefully and told Washington that he would be happy to chat with him while they waited for their flights. It turned out that both of them were on their way to Costa Rica on the same plane. The dark stranger offered to continue their conversation during the flight but added that it would not be gratis; it was going to cost something. Washington was taken aback; he was truly surprised at what the man had said. The deal, explained the stranger, was that Washington would have to put on the tefillin and pray with him. Washington's face turned red, as he had to admit that he had forgotten all about it and had not done it for years since the time of his Bar Mitzvah. The man comforted him and, putting his hand on Washington's shoulder, promised to show him how it was done and to refresh his memory with the right prayers as well.

The plane took off and Washington did not see his new friend for a while. Sitting towards the back of the plane all by himself, with nobody in his row, Washington thought that the man had forgotten all about him. It usually takes three-and-a-half hours to fly from Lima to Costa Rica. About one hour into the flight, the bearded gentleman came over and sat next to Washington. He handed him a tefillin, guided him on the right way to wear it, began praying, and motioned to Washington to do the same. Washington was somewhat concerned about the possible curiosity of other passengers but the plane was half-empty and those sitting nearby did not seem to pay any attention to them. He forgot all about the surroundings as he got absorbed in the prayers, and did not realize how quickly time passed until they were about to reach their destination. The man got up—he was very lean and tall—and looking down at Washington said, before returning to his seat, *"Now you have reached a stage where you will be with God."* Suddenly, the plane abruptly went into a rapid descent. Washington felt somewhat dizzy and closed his eyes for a moment. When he reopened them the plane had landed and the man was gone. As Washington was being greeted by his daughter and her fiancé, he saw the bearded man getting into a large black car driven by an almost identical looking individual. The car rolled off and turned a corner. Washington never saw the man again but he never forgot him either. That incident changed his life.

Back in Santiago, he was fortunate to find and join a most unusual congregation. It is a place of worship where a person feels uplifted by the music, the songs, and by the general feeling of joy that dominates the gatherings. He has learned to worship God in happiness. He has gone back to his roots. He spends the High Holidays in the temple, not always praying but sometimes just meditating or reading. During Yom Kippur, he often cries, remembering all those who have passed on, and he feels redeemed and cleansed. His memories have resurfaced and he is at home with the other members of the congregation and the rabbi whom he admires. It is a dwelling unlike any other synagogue he has visited; it is devoid of the sense of gloom and sadness he has experienced in other places. He recalls his mother who, in spite of their poverty, always managed to have new clothes for him for Rosh Hashanah. He now continues to follow the same custom and always, but always, has a new suit for the holidays. The weather at that time of the year is often unpredictable, sometimes hot and sometimes cold. Hence, he decided that he would get two sets of new clothes, one suit to keep him cool and one to keep him warm, depending on how the weather turns out! The main thing for him is to honor his mother's memory; no matter what he wears, he is Isaac once again.

Source Note

Based on an interview with Washington Domb Scott in Santiago, in March 2002. Washington Domb is a lawyer who lives in Santiago, Chile. He has spent many years in Costa Rica, where his married daughter resides. He had an important job during the regime of Salvador Allende but was jailed for forty-five days when Augusto Pinochet overthrew Allende on Sept.11, 1973. He was then released but expelled from the country to Costa Rica, where he spent over ten years of his life until he was allowed to return.

Text Note

1. In 1503, Columbus landed in what is now Puerto Limon, Costa Rica, on his fourth voyage to the New World. He named the area Costa Rica (Rich Coast), some say, because of the beauty he found there; others say because he had heard rumors of gold. Be that as it may, he was right in the first instance and wrong in the second. It was quickly discovered that there was comparatively little gold, but the natural beauty of Costa Rica has been attracting visitors and settlers ever since its initial colonization (*http://www.costaricaexpeditions.com/aboutcr*).

The House on Back Street

The tourist could not believe his eyes. He had spent about five hours taking night-time pictures of interesting places in an old, residential section of St. Thomas and all of them, despite his first-rate equipment and expertise in photography, had turned out opaque. Other shots taken during the day were just beautiful. The two historic towers—Blackbeard and Bluebeard—named after the seventeenth century notorious pirates Captain Kidd and the Frenchman Jean Hamil, who had "graced" the island with their visit, came out brilliantly, and the rest of the shots in the developed film could be considered truly artistic as well. He scratched his head, puzzled and, despite his disappointment, decided to give it another try the next evening.

St. Thomas was one of the most interesting islands that he had visited in the Caribbean.[1] He was a middle-aged, unattached architect whose hobby was photography and who traveled extensively in search of wondrous and extraordinary sights. He had walked all over the island, ascended its winding hills, enjoyed the many tropical flowers that blanketed the terrain, and delighted in the diversity of creatures found in the open. He stood for hours watching the harbor and taking pictures of the spectacular views nature offered him so generously. From afar he could hear the enticing sound of the local music—the swaying rhythm of steel pans and scratch-bands that were so popular on the island.[2] He loved the way they walked the earth, the friendliness that was imbedded in the people who hailed from so many places in the world, and, maybe just because of that, shared quite a unique style of living and culture.

Later that evening, after feasting on a typical West Indian meal of saltfish, red beans, rice, and plantains, he turned once again towards downtown, his equipment re-checked, in order to explore the buildings and mansions of the island. He had visited the St. Thomas synagogue the previous day and been impressed by the historical site—its sand floor, the ornate interior architecture—and had felt touched remembering his religious paternal grandmother who was Jewish and from whom he had learned about the faith of his forefathers.[3] He had seen most of the important buildings in town, such as the Weibel Museum that depicts the three hundred year history of the Jewish population of the island, the Crown House that used to be the residence of the Governor General of the Danish West Indies in 1822, as well as other places that are considered tourist attractions. Being an architect, such old mansions appealed to him tremendously. Most of all, though, he liked to look at homes that were outstanding, not necessarily due to the status of their former residents or their historical value but rather had a character of their own and a tale to tell.

He walked around for a couple of hours. The air was cool and it was pretty dark since it happened to be a moonless night. He took a number of pictures of various buildings that attracted his attention, some of which seemed not to be inhabited. Finally, tired and ready to start his walk back to the hotel, he noticed a large, tall stone house on the hillside of a road named Back Street. The windows were dark on all of the four floors and the terraces that ran along each of them looked abandoned. It had a peculiar appearance, not like a mansion or a home but rather more like a stern monastery or convent. He wondered to whom it belonged but there was nobody around he could ask. He saw only a weatherworn mailbox with no name posted, yet noticed a small Star of David engraved on it. He shrugged his shoulders and decided to take a few pictures before leaving. Initially his camera would not respond; it seemed to be frozen and the flash went off a few times for no particular reason. In the end, he managed to take a few shots and left the place annoyed, angry at his equipment, grunting and muttering to himself that such a thing had never, ever happened to him. The next day when he had his photos developed, all came out well except those of the house on Back Street. Disgusted, he was about to toss those lightless misfits into the wastebasket when he noticed that one of the pictures had some fuzzy outlines in it. He could not figure out what they were, so he took it to the photo laboratory and asked the technician to work on it, lightening it as much as possible. After a while, a clerk handed it back to him with a strange smile on his face. He gasped when he opened the envelope; in the dim background of the photo he saw about five squiggly images that looked rather misty, but a strange light seemed to radiate from somewhere, surrounding them with an odd aura. He was far from being a superstitious man but there was no doubt about it, he must have taken a picture of some ghosts!

The next day he returned to Back Street to investigate. The sun was shining brightly and the house did not look as ominous as it had the previous moonless night. He felt somewhat embarrassed to have come back in search of some supernatural creatures. He passed a few Mango and Genep trees along the way that were typical, deciduous tropical fruit trees that grew on the island and paused for a while under a huge Lignum tree. It was getting quite warm and he was sweating. He looked up and saw clusters of large fruit hanging from the branches. A couple of them detached themselves and hit him on his hat. "I guess," he thought, "the spirits don't want me to come back . . ." mocking himself although deep down in his heart he felt that things were not really what they seemed. A woman carrying a basket on a *catta*—the protective head cushion created from a sack—passed by without looking at him. He called out and asked if she knew who lived in the house on Back Street. She stopped for a while and told him that it was uninhabited right then but that years ago a large Jewish family, by the name of Sasso, had lived there. They had been well off but prone to tragedies: the reason being that the house used to be a Catholic rectory that was erected next to a graveyard in the previous century and where many morbid things had happened. She could not give him any more details, though, and suggested he find a Mocko Jumbie who frequented the marketplace and who knew all about the island's tales.[4] Knowing that the Mocko Jumbies were stilt dancers who represented ancient African healers and protectors from evil spirits—wearing a mask and colorful clothes—he decided that it was, most probably, the best person who could give him an insight into the mystery of the house on Back Street.

It was not difficult to find the Mocko Jumbie; the locals directed him to a small, narrow house close to the marketplace. The Mocko Jumbie was at home and invited him in, offering him a chair and a cold tamarind drink lightly spiced with rum. The stilts were leaning on a wall and the small, lean man was not wearing a mask since he was not performing but just resting at home. When asked about the house on Back Street, he did not seem surprised, since curiosity and superstition are considered natural on the island and not necessarily a negative aspect of human nature.

Years ago the sturdy building had been a rectory and housed many nuns and a few priests. One of the clergy was a vicious man who forced himself on the nuns and impregnated some of them. Locals tell that in order to keep his depraved deeds secret, he buried the unborn or newborn babies either in the adjacent graveyard or under the basement of the seminary. The Sasso family purchased the house around 1859 and did some remodeling but the basic appearance remained and so did all the ghosts that haunted the premises—all the forlorn souls of those that had not found peace and others that joined them over the years. The Jewish owner of the house, a man named Abraham Sasso, with his wife Leah and their ten children lived on the top floor while some of their relatives and a number of servants occupied the rest of the mansion. Leah Sasso was a gentle lady and very busy taking care of the household. She kept many of her supplies in a large pantry and preferred to keep an eye on it herself, since she was in charge of the provisions. She noticed, shortly after they moved in, that each time she opened the door to the storeroom, a cold sensation overtook her and caused her to get goose bumps. She dismissed her discomfort, assuming that cold air was a good thing since it would keep the food supplies in the pantry fresh and make them last for a long time. One day, though, Elvina, a young servant who had been brought up by Leah, found her passed out inside the pantry. Leah did recover, but refused to go near the storeroom anymore and handed the keys to her housekeeper without any explanation. From then on things went downhill. The servant, while entering the pantry, encountered, on several occasions, the translucent image of a man who looked like the deceased husband of one of the relatives who lived on the second floor and whose big, white, hairy arms tried to clasp her throat. The rest of the staff believed her and thought that the ghost might have also been the vile priest who had taken the form of the dead master. Addie, the housekeeper, a mulatto woman who had come from the island of St. Croix, refused to accept the explanation and reprimanded the mortified young servant for making up tall tales. She changed her mind, however, one dismal December night, when she saw a gray-green mist coming out of the pantry and a rather foul stench, much like the odor of rotting flesh, engulfed her. The door of the pantry began rattling as if somebody or something was trying to break it down, bottles of marmalade and guava jellies were swept off the cabinet as if by a big invisible hand, and a tall, white man with fiery eyes, holding a severed, bleeding head of an infant, tried to block Addie's way. She fled the room and later on, when she recovered and went back to find out what had really happened, found only the smashed bottles and jars on the floor but no sign of even a drop of the blood that she had seen dripping slowly but surely from the dangling head. Following that event, the pantry was sealed tight and nobody ever used it again. Things, though, never calmed down at the mansion on Back Street; spirit phenomena were very frequent and there were reports that silent, solemn ghosts came out of all the wall closets, particularly on full moonlit nights.

The Mocko Jumbie finished his narrative about the House on Back Street and smiled politely as he watched his guest's face. The architect was silent for a while but then got up and thanked the old man in whose company he had spent a most memorable afternoon in St. Thomas. He hesitated for a moment when the stilt artist offered to provide him with an amulet that would enable proper photos to be taken of the House on Back Street. The Mocko Jumbie took it as an affirmative answer and, searching for something in his closet, came up with a string of seven blue crystals with a red one in the middle. He said that those were the stones favored by Yemeya, the Goddess of the Moon, and that anyone wearing the necklace could approach evil spirits of the night without fear since it prevented them from harming the person or interfering with any-thing he or she wanted to do.[5] The architect gracefully declined the offer, particularly since he had no intention of returning to the mansion on

Back Street. The one and only odd picture he had of the house he kept on a separate page in his St. Thomas album and, for some reason, never showed it to any of his friends.

Source Note

Based on a letter written by David Stanley Sasso of St. Thomas to his cousin Cheryl Pinto of Colon, Panama. David Stanley Sasso was born into a respected and prominent Sephardic Jewish family on the island. He was a highly educated man, devoted to the history of his people as well as the folklore of the island he loved. During his lifetime, he personally experienced many supernatural psychic phenomena and was regarded by the native people as a person of great insight and unusual powers. His love for the local lore induced him to personify a legendary woman who used to frequent the market in the 1940s and told tales while selling sweets. David Stanley Sasso, thus, dressed up in colorful women's clothes and imitating Martha, the market woman, became a well-known figure in downtown St. Thomas. His performance was extraordinary and he released a cassette in 1986, and later a video, that, together with a book of folktales, brought him fame. All this was commendable especially since he was a sixty-year-old widower, disabled, and half blind. He passed away in 1996 and is buried in the Jewish Cemetery in St. Thomas.

Text Notes

1. The Island of St Thomas – Columbus discovered St. Thomas in 1493 and since then the island has changed hands many times. It was for a long time a trade center for slaves and a convenient enclave for piracy. Spain, Malta, France, England, Holland, and Denmark owned St. Thomas at various times; finally, the island was purchased by the United States from Denmark in 1917, during World War I, and developed into a military base. Today, it serves, just as many of the other Virgin Islands, as a popular vacation place.

2. The origin of the music – Steel pans and scratch-bands go back to the days when conventional instruments were not readily available and the poor but very ingenious musicians instead used washboards, pans, various kinds of gourds, and ukulele- and flute-like instruments to compose their own original, folk melodies (*http://www.virginisles.com/culture.html*).

3. The St. Thomas synagogue – Founded in 1796, the temple was burned down three times and each time rebuilt. The present building goes back to the year 1833. The sand floor is in memory of the days of the Spanish Inquisition when the devout Jews, afraid to be discovered, had to pray in basements and be careful to muffle the sound of their feet. Another explanation is that it is meant

to commemorate the forty years Israelites wandered in the desert. Other temples in the Caribbean also have sand on their floors, the oldest one being the famous synagogue in Curacao.

4. Mocko Jumbies – An ancient African art form is performed by *Mocko Jumbies*, mostly men who engage in a cultural dance standing on stilts, wearing masks and traditional clothing. Their height symbolically represents the power of gods and their greatness, and they serve as spiritual protectors of their people. They never disclose their identity, covering their faces with masks and their clothes with small mirrors that are supposed to frighten evil spirits who cannot bear to look at their own images. The African slaves brought such religious traditions to the Caribbean and they have been part of the Virgin Islands' culture for over two hundred years *(http://www.st-thomas.com/jumbies/Mocko_Jumbie_History.htm)*.

5. Santeria is a religious practice that African slaves brought to the Americas. It centers on ancient African gods, such as Yemeya, some who have in time been assimilated as Catholic saints. "Santeria" comes from the Spanish word "Santo," meaning saint, and is popular in the Caribbean Basin.

The Coffee Party

San Telmo is one of the oldest barrios of Buenos Aires.[1] In this place the city of Santa Maria of Buenos Aires was founded in 1570 by Juan de Garay.[2] In the 1930s, San Telmo was a crowded area that many immigrants from various parts of the world called home. Among those were many Jews that had arrived from European countries, most of them Ashkenazi, but also quite a large number of Sephardic Jews from diverse areas such as Turkey, Macedonia, the Greek Islands, and parts of Africa. Most of them were the descendants of the Marranos that had fled the Inquisition in Spain and Portugal in the fifteenth century.

In the first decades of the twentieth century there existed in San Telmo some exclusive, rambling, big homes that belonged to the wealthy, but most dwellings along the narrow streets and passages were humbler and less prominent. These were the typical "casas chorizos" of those times, elongated structures of one or two stories with a central shady patio. The front of the house, the portico, was decorated with Italian moldings. These were much like the homes of the Romans in olden times and also some of the more contemporary Mediterranean buildings. It was in Jewish households of this kind that typical afternoon parties took place almost every other day of the week when women, who were friends and acquaintances, sat down in the cool area of the courtyard and enjoyed coffee or tea. These were sessions to "adulsar" or sweeten the day, where women sampled various desserts and discussed families and events that had transpired. Many women were young and loved to listen to the tales that the older members of this "chat" club could tell them. One such group was more fortunate than the others since they had among them two ladies who were very good storytellers and could enhance the sweetness of their get-togethers with tales from the old countries. These two grandmothers of a young boy named José loved to share with their friends the memories they had cherished for years.

José remembers those gatherings, since as a child he used to observe the guests, listen to the stories, and enjoy the sweets. It was very common in those days to live with the grandparents; many members of the family shared a house and the intimate events of every single day. These special surroundings had a magic of their own and this unusual enchantment left a powerful impact on José's childhood remembrances. Today, a grandfather himself, he recalls with nostalgia and a touch of sadness mixed with admiration the relations that existed between people in those past days. Being an architect, he is able to "reconstruct" the customs of the daily lives of long ago and the anecdotes of the grandmothers that had a very essential historical core mingled with personal experiences and deep feelings.

José's grandfathers, unfortunately, had passed away before he was born and, thus, he does not remember them; but he has a vivid picture of his grandmothers. José's paternal grandmother, Myriam, lived with the family in their house and his maternal grandmother, Esther, in a small apartment a few blocks away. Myriam's family had come from the island of Rhodes, while Esther was a native of Smyrna, Turkey.[3] Both women had a strong mutual tie with their Sephardic roots that went back all the way to Spain and in their attachment to ancient traditions that they practiced with zest. They were, however, very different in some ways, particularly in their looks. Myriam had the dark hair and intense black eyes of a typical Sephardic beauty, while Esther, surprisingly, had thick, blond strands and heavenly blue eyes. These characteristics she passed on to her daughter, José's mother, from whom he inherited them as well. They were always admired for those features by other members of their congregation and jokingly teased as being Ashkenazi "infiltrators," since their coloring was quite different from that of the typical Sephardic people.

Myriam was a wonderful cook and Esther was not far behind her. They exercised their culinary talents in many dishes that were typically Turkish with a Jewish touch. José's mouth always waters as he remembers the *Yaprakes* that, like the Greek dolmas, were a delicacy. His grandmothers cooked the humble cabbage, then filled the translucent leaves with sautéed rice, pine nuts, and currants, mixed with many secret spices and herbs, and served them in a beautiful dish decorated with lemon wedges. This was presented at times with a soup called *shorva* that was similar to the Turkish corba with pieces of meat in it. A salad of cucumbers and a yogurt dressing with some *kashkaval* cheese was also accompanied with *burrakitas,* which are the famous philo dough pockets, fried or baked, stuffed with fillings of many kinds. The meal also included a pudding made of milk or water called *malebi,* equivalent of the Turkish dish *muhallebi.* The cuisine of Rhodes included these dishes as well, and they also used many meat dishes, mainly lamb, heavily spiced with garlic. The family enjoyed a variety of divine desserts such as different kinds of baklava, halva, and other sweets that were more typically Sephardic and served on special occasions.

The afternoon coffee parties were quite simple as far as the sweets were concerned. The main purpose was the conversation, and the desserts were more symbolic than anything else, just to enlighten and enhance the routine of every day tasks and events. The grandmothers served the sweets on a fancy, shiny, oval silver tray. There were usually three kinds of sweets: those made with rose water, others from the skin of the bitter orange (*naranja marga*) with the bitterness removed, and, the most typical, the *sharope*, made from pure syrup with the most intense sugary flavor. In the center of the tray were placed about a dozen small spoons. Each person chose a sweet with a spoon and then washed it off with a glass of water that was an absolute necessity since the flavor was so strong. They also drank Turkish coffee or, at times, tea. Coffee was the favorite, an almost addictive habit of the women; it was served in a pot with a long handle and always frothy and aromatic. It was taken boiled, strong or medium, and with or without sugar. The cups with the very sweet coffee were placed in the tray, with the handles pointing outwards; the cups with coffee that was less sweet were arranged so that the handles were at an angle towards the center of the tray. The cups without any sugar had their handles pointed directly inwards. Sometimes they added fragrant substances such as a little cardamom, jasmine, cloves, or a few drops of rose water. The ceremonial art of serving the coffee had an additional element of entertainment, particularly for the non-Jewish friends who were at times invited. Some of the women liked to turn the empty coffee cups upside down on the saucer; after waiting a few minutes, one of them, the designated fortune teller, would read the patterns on the saucer and predict the future. This custom survived for a long time, although it was not necessarily typical among the Sephardic Jews. Their extremely versatile and rich food has been passed on from one generation to the next without any difficulty. Things change over time because of different and multiple factors but the culinary customs are kept and seem to be a most important component of the structure of a people. It is almost an inescapable legacy.

Myriam and Esther were exceptional not only as cooks but also as tellers of tales. Myriam could trace the history of her family for centuries, since the expulsion from Spain, to the Juderiiya, the Jewish quarter of the island of Rhodes. This fascinating island, which the geographer Strabo called the most beautiful place on earth, had been home to the first Sephardim, early victims of the Inquisition who arrived in Rhodes in the beginning of the thirteenth century.[4] The Jewish quarter had been located close to the harbor and, in time, became a colorful place—its streets full of homes and shops of the rich and the poor who, nevertheless, created a community that lived in harmony. The people had the reputation of being diligent merchants, gifted musicians who had composed many Ladino ballads and *romanceros*, and their women beautiful, high-spirited, excellent cooks, and embroiders. Myriam often retold the legend of the Colossus of Rhodes, one of the seven marvels of the world, erected at the harbor in the fifth century B.C. in the honor of Helios, the God of Sun.[5] The ancient people believed that their island was particularly blessed for that reason, and their favorite proverb was that the sun shone everyday on Rhodes.

Conditions, however, were not always favorable for the Jews; they lived through many difficult periods and had to cope with economic as well as social problems. Myriam's son, José's father, was born in Rhodes in 1900 and, when he grew up, intended to sail to France to study, since proper education was a difficult issue for Jews on the island in those days. He was not able to accomplish his goal because the ship that was going to take him out of Rhodes sank and there were no other means of transportation available. José's father studied on his own and became an autodidact, a self-educated person, knowledgeable in many fields. When he immigrated to Argentina in the early 1920s, he became a very respected member of the community in Buenos Aires. He founded the Temple Shalom in 1922, in honor of the synagogue in Rhodes that carried the same name and to which he always had a very strong spiritual connection.

Esther's stories were based in Smyrna, where her family had resided for generations. She recounted the tale of how her forefathers had left Spain in a hurry, leaving their belongings, all that they had built in that country, so that they would not have to give up their heritage. Fear was also a dominant factor that drove thousands of them out of the country around 1492, following their eviction by Queen Isabella and King Ferdinand of Spain. So many Sephardic Jews were shipping out of Cadiz and Seville that Columbus, who was ready to embark on one of his famous voyages to the New World, had to depart from a different, less crowded seaport. When the Jews reached the Ottoman Empire, they were welcomed by the benign Sultan Bayazid II, who gave them new hope, assistance, and encouragement.[6] The Sultan did not have much regard for King Ferdinand's judgment; he predicted the impoverishment of Spain due to the expulsion of the Jews and could foresee the advantage they would bring to his country.

Esther's father had been a coachman in Smyrna and immigrated to Argentina in 1898; this was rather early compared to most of the Sephardic Jews who came to the New World much later than the Ashkenazis. Thus, Esther was perhaps one of the first Sephardic women to come to Argentina. Her father, though, had not left his homeland forever; he took the whole family back on a nostalgic trip to the old country. The visit lasted five years, since they arrived there at the onset of World War I and were unable to leave Europe until the war ended. The timing was bad but Esther, nevertheless, had some very beautiful memories that went back to that period in her life. Smyrna, or the modern Izmir as it is called now, is an enticing place, famous for its connections to many myths of the ancient world and to several civilizations that originated in the Aegean part of the world. It is also a most beautiful city that lies at the head of a narrow and long gulf that feels more like an enormous blue lake than a sea since the waters are very calm. Esther's family lived along the Bay of Smyrna, in the quarter of Karatash that still does exist. Their house, similar to the one they owned later in Argentina, faced the water. At the end of their patio, there was a ladder along which they could descend straight into the sea; each household had a private access and could enjoy the waters to their hearts' content. The climate was mild and in the summer the sea breezes were not only constant but also refreshing, since they tempered the sun's heat. In those days, things were simple; there was no refrigeration and in order to enjoy certain foods, the families had a special system. They loved to eat *sandia,* the watermelon, and used to put it into a net and slowly lower it into the sea where it would be left for a few hours until it was very cold and extremely tasty. Esther had never eaten a watermelon as delicious as the ones they used to have in Smyrna.

Upon their return to Argentina, Esther's father and his brothers started a business in San Telmo. It was a shoe store that served the general population of the quarter as well as many sailors who came to the port and were looking for everyday necessities. When a ship docked at the port, the shop usually stayed open until midnight. Esther liked to tell the story of how, in that very shop, José's father saw her daughter for the first time and fell in love. Their courtship was very romantic and they had a very happy marriage that lasted many years. José was the first-born, followed by two younger sisters. Esther did not like to dwell on the fact that, despite their happy family life, there was a toll taken not just by old age but also the harsh Argentinean climate and dirty, polluted river waters. Conditions in the early days were very bad, medical care was primitive, and they did not always know why or from what their family members died. Esther always finished her stories with a joke or an interesting, amusing anecdote she had heard just the day before. Laughter was a very important part of life and she never gave it up.

Coffee parties might still take place in some family quarters but many old traditions to which the previous generations were attached have disappeared. They are undermined by a growing trend of assimilation and modernization of social life. Maybe only a very few of the old traditions—such as the culinary ones—are still practiced and known to the young generations, but they will not perish as long as the memory of these events and customs is saved in tales. Walking along the crowded streets of San Telmo these days, next to the countless antique shops and restaurants, the hustle and bustle of a modern, dynamic place takes over. However, while watching the tango dancers in the plaza, one can still imagine the two grandmothers in their prime, whirling around with their husbands, their spirits safe and sound.[7]

Source Note

Based on an interview with José Tarica in Buenos Aires, March 2002. José's family name Tarica is not of Italian origin as many seem to think but an interesting combination of Arabic and Hebrew roots. In the seventh century, a warrior by the name of Tariq-ibn-Ziyad crossed from North Africa to Spain at a place that is today called Gibraltar. The rock was named after him, Jabal Tarik, meaning the Mountain of the Path, for the path of Islam into the Iberian Peninsula. As time went by the name was mispronounced and morphed into Gibraltar. The Hebrew component comes from the same roots: *madrich*—a guide, and from there to the word—*adrichal*—an architect, which is exactly what José Tarica is.

Text Notes

1. Barrio – quarter
2. Juan de Garay (1528–1583), a Spanish explorer and conqueror, participated in various operations in Peru and Bolivia and became the governor of the River of the Plata area in 1576. A year later he re-founded the city of Buenos Aires that had originally been founded in 1536 by Pedro de Mendoza. It had been a fort that was given the name of "Our Lady of Good Air" and destroyed later by the Indians. The second, legal foundation of the city was laid on June 11, 1580, in the place that was later called San Telmo and Monserrat.
3. The Jews of Rhodes trace their ancestry to Genesis. The island is mentioned in the book and there is proof that there existed a Jewish settlement in the first century and St. Paul had visited it. Later, the crusaders captured the island and built the fortress, and the Jews lived within its walls for centuries until the Ottomans Turks conquered it in 1522. After World War I, the island became a part of Italy. When, with the fall of Mussolini, the island was taken over by the Germans, most Jews were sent to Auschwitz and today there are only a handful left. The oldest synagogue, Kahal Shalom (built in 1577), still stands there.

4. Strabo, the geographer, was born in 64 or 63 B.C. in the city of Amaseia (now called Amasya), capital of Pontus, a region in northeastern Anatolia that was an independent kingdom from the fourth century B.C. until it was captured by Rome in 66 B.C. The seventeen volumes of his *Geographika* provide information on the geography of the ancient world stretching from the Atlantic Ocean in the west to the Indus River in the east.

5. Colossus of Rhodes, a 105 ft high bronze statue honoring Apollo or Helios, was made in 290 B.C. by the sculptor Chares of Lindos, a native of the island, and erected at the entrance to the harbor. The monstrous giant, with its legs spread wide apart, was so huge that the largest ship with its sails spread out, as legends claim, could move into the harbor underneath it. It collapsed in 223 B.C. due to an earthquake, and the metal was supposedly sold to a Jewish merchant. And when it fell, it was so enormous that "few people could make their arms meet round the thumb," wrote Pliny, the Roman historian (23 A.D.–79 A.D.). The colossus disappeared but this towering ancient statue inspired modern artists such as French sculptor Auguste Bartholdi, best known for his famous work, the Statue of Liberty.

6. Turkey – Jews have always enjoyed the beneficence and good will tradition- ally displayed by the Turkish government and the tolerance of its people towards different creeds, cultures, and races. Over the centuries a large number of European Jews, escaping persecution in their native countries, settled in the Ottoman Empire. Sources: *Encyclopedia Judaica* and H. Graetz's *History of the Jews*.

7. The Tango – Toward the mid-nineteenth century, this famous dance emerged in the inner city of Buenos Aires, with the formation of new social class that consisted of peasants who came from the inland, European immi- grants, and disadvantaged *porteños* (born in Buenos Aires). They wanted to identify themselves as a group in their new home and the tango became a mani- festation of a new culture.

The Medic

The village of Nova Stolitsa consisted of two narrow streets—that was it—yet more than half a million people consider it their beloved little shtetele. This tiny dot on the map of Europe, from where many people began their journey toward freedom, was at different times part of Bessarabia, Romania, Russia, or Transylvania. The locals there were so helpful, their hearts so very full of compassion as well as courage, that even those who just passed through it were engulfed in all that empathy and sympathy. The grateful escapees decided from then on to tell others that it was their hometown as well. The children and grandchildren of those who were saved also became loyal adopted sons and daughters.

This is where the doctor's story starts, in 1926, when his eighteen-year-old father escaped from Romania to avoid being drafted into the Russian army. The fate of the Jews who were forced to join was grim and their future many times non-existent or bleak at best. Upon his arrival in Peru, Jacobo's father was fortunate to locate a relative who had been living there for some time and who helped him out until he was able to stand on his own feet. Life was very hard, and the fairy tales of the Amazon, as the land where gold could be found on the streets, were quickly forgotten with the hardships of everyday life. Jacobo's mother arrived as a bride within a short time and the young couple labored together to make their living. Reality continued to be very different from what they had initially envisioned. The father established himself as a peddler and traveled all over the country and even outside of its borders. Once, while in Colombia, he contracted malaria and had to return to Lima and nearly died. Fortunate to survive, he decided to find a permanent place for himself and his wife, a place where they could start a family. Cajabamba, to the north of Lima, had a good reputation for business and that is where they moved.

Cajabamba is located about three thousand meters above sea level;

its landscape is full of geographical diversity, mountains, fertile valleys, forests, and lakes. The uneven hue of greenery changes from one area to another and the rocks hide the remains of ancient towns from the remote pre-Hispanic times. Close to Cajabamba, mainly in Cajamarka and Otusco, and in some other small towns, there dwelled at that time just a few Jewish families. Their ancestors had lived there since the seventeenth and eighteenth centuries, and the children and grandchildren of those early settlers left the area only toward the end of the nineteenth and the early twentieth centuries. Some of them made *aliyah*—immigration to Israel—while others moved to Lima. There are almost no Jews left in those towns today.

Jacobo's father, as other Jewish peddlers of those days, used to attend many fairs and travel from one to the next. The festivals had open markets and were a very good source of income for the merchants. Most of these events were in honor of patron saints, each on a particular day within the Christian calendar, as had been decided during the Vice-Regency. However, all observances also incorporated the magical and superstitious beliefs of each region in the country. It was, and still is, the worship of the sacred and the profane intertwined, where the manifestation of the Peruvian spirit comes together. It is a show of the people's artistic ability, their vitality, joy of life, and pride. The Spanish priests had long ago introduced the portable *retablos,* which were initially altars used by the people of the Andes to house the statues of the saints they honored. The farmers and shepherds of alpacas brought them into towns to celebrate the harvest and the shearing of the animals. The Jewish peddlers were welcomed on these occasions by the native people who, despite their acute poverty, always knew how to rejoice and enjoy the small pleasures of life. It was a simple life for the peddlers, full of strife but very different from the one they experienced in Europe. Diseases were quite common and hard to treat due to lack of proper medical facilities. Francisco Pizarro had brought with him not only greed and a reign of terror but also unknown, fatal diseases that the local population had not encountered earlier. One of Jacobo's younger siblings died of diphtheria for that very reason.

It might be that the tragedy of his little brother's death, perhaps with other motives, triggered Jacobo's interest in medicine at a young age. When the children grew up, Jacobo's parents moved to Lima. Many Jewish families changed their place of residence to the city—where there was a big Jewish community—in order to lessen the chances of their children marrying gentiles. Jacobo studied medicine in the Peruvian capital and then got his training in the United States. He lived for five years in New York and then moved back to Lima, where he built a big hospital as well as a smaller clinic. When life became difficult because of political upheavals, he and his family left and settled down in Miami. In 1999, though, despite the fact that his children remained in the States, he and his wife decided to go back to Lima, where Jacobo continues to practice general surgery and where they have lived ever since.

Highly respected in the Jewish community as a doctor and their former president, Jacobo is also very knowledgeable about history. In 1870, a few German Jews founded the Jewish Society. Those were the first Jews, since the time of the conquistadores, who did not hide their identity in fear of the Inquisition. In the past Jews had prayed in an underground synagogue in Lima, the location of which was kept secret. A hidden Jew from the court of the Viceroy, by the name of Leon Pinelo, had made it possible. There also exists an urban legend about an ancient scroll that was given to the community in 1937. That year, in a local store, some Jews were discussing the sad reality that they did not have a Torah in their place of worship. A certain person overheard them talking, approached them, and told them that he happened to have, in one of his old trunks, a scroll that looked exactly like the object they were interested in. He invited them to his house and—lo and behold—a Torah it was! They have it in their synagogue till today. Nobody knows where the scroll came from. The person who donated it had a German name but he regarded himself as a gentile since his father had married a non-Jewish woman who never converted. The German Jews were highly educated and did not care to associate with the Polish, Romanian, and other people who came from Europe. They remained aloof and the divisions grew even more as many Jews arrived from such countries as Turkey and Morocco and founded a

Sephardic community of their own. The gap was so vast that intermarriage between a Sephardic and Ashkenazi family was considered a bigger disaster than marriage to a gentile. At a certain time there existed about ten synagogues in Lima and there were close to six thousand five hundred worshipping Jews.

In 1940, the societies came to their senses and, despite the fact that they continued praying in separate houses of worship, decided to become one big Jewish community. It became a very unusual and outgoing organization. Shops opened one next to another, people in need were well taken care of, and those who asked for support in order to start a business were offered loans and encouraged to become independent. In the evenings they met in coffeehouses to chat and discuss different issues. The ties became very close, children attended clubs like the Maccabi and Hanoar Hatzione, everybody knew everybody, and life was good. They seemed to enjoy the simple things in life, they trusted each other, and a call for help was answered without even asking for the name of the person; it was enough to know that he was a Jew. The happy times did not last long though. Human nature is quite predictable and once some members of the community became rich, while others remained poor, a division arose between those who had plenty and those who had very little. On top of that, there also emerged a division based on whether a person was a Sephardic ("Schwarze" or Black) Jew or an Ashkenazi ("Wiesse" or White), and the gap widened once again. This cycle happened a few times, but it was the Ashkenazi community that had a better grip and understanding for what the future might hold. The next generation became more literate; doctors, lawyers and, engineers emerged, and prosperity again knocked at the doors. It is quite unusual for a community to split apart and get back together so many times for a variety of reasons. Most of the native Peruvians, on the other hand, were consistently very gracious, accepted the Jews willingly, and made them feel at home.

Some of the Jews in Lima contributed to the welfare of the country. A man from France, Henry Mieggs, who arrived in Peru around 1880, considered himself Jewish and became famous for building the Oryoa railroad from Lima to Guancayo, which is an amazing accomplishment. It is the highest in the world and lifts itself up to almost sixteen thousand feet elevation in an unbelievably short distance. Mieggs engineered an unusual bridge that spans two tunnels over a precipice that is a thousand feet deep and which is called with affection El Infiernillo—the Little Hell. It is a ride through the clouds of heaven with the fear of hell in one's heart. Mieggs also founded the Jewish cemetery in Lima where a Jew by the name of Zehnder was the first to be buried.

Sadly, Zehnder's children and grandchildren denied their Jewish origins and his is just another forgotten grave. If he had known, he might have found solace in the fact that there are many people in Peru today who believe that they are the descendants of the "Ten Lost Tribes of Israel," and whose ancestors are not necessarily buried in Jewish cemeteries. It might have warmed his heart if he had believed, as the saying goes, that, "A Jewish soul is always a Jewish soul," no matter what.

Jacobo does not dwell on death for too long. His eyes light up when he mentions his grandchildren and it is quite obvious that he loves children, and not just those who have been fortunate to belong to his family. His heart goes out to the little beggars who roam the streets of Peruvian towns and villages but who, despite their bitter fate, have a sense of joy and honor that does not dissipate. He talks about the small storytellers of Arequipa (in the Sierra) who approach people and offer to tell a tale of horror for a coin. When the surprised visitor agrees, a tiny child begins the tale of an avalanche of rocks that descended on his village during an earthquake, killing many people within moments. He stops short, at that point, and sadly comments that, being so young, he does not know the rest of the tale. A bigger boy takes his place and, after asking for his share and given the extra coin, continues describing the terrible events until he also stops and lets another older friend continue. It sometimes takes as many as seven or eight children to finish their storytelling session but they earn the money and do not ask for handouts just for being poor. The little storytellers at times diversify and offer to take pictures of the tourists for a small fee; they tell people how to stand, check the background carefully and, with a big grin, ask them to smile as they call out: "W.H.I.S.K.Y!"

I looked for little storytellers while visiting some villages in the Sierra but for some reason did not find them. The only conversation I had with a little shepherd boy in one of those places was very short; he told me the name of his two llamas, how old they were, and how much he cared for them. He did not offer to take a picture of us but let me take one of him, smiling broadly in his colorful poncho and hugging his beloved alpacas.

Source Note

Based on an interview with Dr. Jacobo Kapilivsky in Lima, Peru, August 2001.

The Shunned Toadstool

Mycological Anti-Semitism

$\mathcal{I}$n the past, fungi were often regarded with suspicion and fear. Mysterious and magical qualities were associated with their unusual shape, and it was also well known that many of the species could be toxic and even fatal. The fact that they thrive in dark and wet places added to the misgivings people held about them. These weird botanical wonders were given strange names that were supported by folklore and superstition. Even when scientific and rational explanations emerged in time, certain stories prevailed and still appear in their old garb.

Myriads of mushrooms spring up all over the world; they sprout, bloom, burst forth, and wither very quickly; some of them have become well known for their poisonous, deadly attributes, yet others—the edibles ones—are considered delicacies, fit to be the food of the gods. Most mushrooms have always been treated with great respect for these reasons, but no fungus has been considered as vile and as unholy as the edible *Auricularia auricula,* or as it is known by its alternate name, *Auricula Judae*—Latin for *Jew's ear*.[1]

The Auricula grows mainly, but not exclusively, on dead and dying elders and its nickname goes back to the Middle Ages. People believed that Judas Iscariot, who had betrayed Jesus for thirty pieces of silver, grew desolate and morbid because of his deed, discarded the money, and hanged himself on an elder tree. The fungus appeared on the tree as a symbolic manifestation of Judas' evil deed, as a representation of his doomed spirit that cannot find rest. The toadstool is edible, velvety soft, and jelly-like, and truly looks like a wrinkled, disfigured ear. Its vicious reputation does not prevent some people from picking it and consuming it in a stew, despite the fact that it does not seem to add any desirable flavor. Some who like practical jokes might enjoy the surprise and disgust on the faces of their guests when they serve the soup that seems to have ears floating in it.

Hatred and hostility towards Jews was widespread, deep and illogical. People forgot that Jesus himself had been a Jew and that Judas, whose exact motives are unknown, had betrayed a friend and not a member of a different religion or race. Judas' act is but one of the excuses for the spread of discrimination, prejudice, and intolerance. Folklore sometimes, as in this case, reinforces the strong negative feelings of those who chose to follow the dark paths. The unlucky Auricula Judae is regarded as cursed, not just because of its shape but also due to its repulsive odor that was believed to have some connection with witchcraft. It grows very quickly and some tales connect its unusual rapid birth and demise with the full moon and the thundering skies. Thunder is usually followed by rain and thus creates the ideal breading field for mushrooms, while the full moon exerts a certain additional gravitational pull to which fungi seem to respond by maturing even faster.

The elder tree shares some of this toadstool's despicable reputation since its flowers and leaves are commonly considered to be foul smelling. That curse fell on the tree since, some say, it was its wood that served as Jesus' cross.[2] This legend has even more far-reaching, dismal insinuations. It was believed that God punished the Jews for Judas' betrayal by inflicting on them the same putrid smell and some abominable diseases. Yet another sinister tale sprang forth as a result of the previous one, claiming that for the Jews the best medicine to combat those illnesses was the blood of Christian children. Thus, it became a common conviction that Jews murdered youngsters particularly around Passover. The proof of the crime—the brownish-reddish flakes that appear on the surface of the baked matzah eaten during the holiday, a sure sign that blood is used in its making. This preposterous, concocted tale, despite its absurdity, was used for generations to compound the suffering of the Jews.

Source Note

Based on an interview with Maxine Lowy in Santiago, Chile, March 2002.

Maxine's father, a professor of Botany at the University of Louisiana, Baton Rouge, was a mycologist and recounted the story in a letter he had written to her. Professor Lowy was born in New York of Hungarian parents. Much of his professional career was oriented toward and spent in the forests of Latin America, including the Amazons, which he visited on several occasions to collect specimens. He passed away in 1992. Maxine Lowy is a human rights activist and a journalist who was born in the United States and now resides in Chile.

Text Notes

1. The origin of the name *Auricula Judae* is Biblical (Mark 3:19). It became a part of medieval European folklore and references to it appear even in such places as Shakespeare's *Love's Labor Lost*. Other mushrooms, in spite of the fact that many have benign medicinal qualities, also do not fare well in folklore. There is an interesting mycological tale related to St. Peter. Once, while he was following Jesus on a country road and eating a piece of bread, he lost few crumbs here and there, which turned into edible mushrooms. However, the devil, who was not far behind him, spat on them and they became beautiful, brightly colored but poisonous toadstools.

2. The elder tree (*Sambucus*) has its share of ugly tales, yet it is actually quite unlikely that its wood served in the manufacture of Jesus' cross since it is a small, very bushy tree (*http://www.culham.info/EasterGarden/elder*; *http://www.istrianet.org/istria/flora/mush-myth*